THE SECRET TO BEING YOU!

Using Brain Science & the 9 Acknowledgment Languages™ to Unbox Your Enneagram

JEN P HIGGINS

Oliver Golden Publishing

To the Difference Makers
in pursuit of your calling,
one self-aware moment at a time.

CONTENTS

Foreword

By Kim Eddy

If we observe ourselves truthfully and non-judgmentally, seeing the mechanisms of our personality in action, we can wake up, and our lives can be a miraculous unfolding of beauty and joy.

- Don Richard Riso,
The Wisdom of the Enneagram

When I first became aware that the Enneagram framework existed, I was pretty desperate for something to change. I felt unseen, unheard, and unmoored from myself. I was in a place where my closest relationships felt foreign to me, and I felt like a stranger to myself, not knowing why I was reacting to life's struggles the way I was, and needing some real, tangible answers.

I was stuck in a personality box of my own (unconscious) making, and I was frustrated with being cooped up in my patterns, habits, and coping mechanisms. I needed a framework that would help me untangle and decipher how I had gotten to where I was. Enter the Enneagram!

The Enneagram helped give language to my deepest motivations, helped me get to know myself more fully, and offered me the self-awareness I needed to start responding intentionally to life — instead of simply reacting blindly to it. I was able to unfurl as a person, exit my long and winding road of confusion, and emerge understanding what made me, well, me.

I attribute much of my growth during that season of my life to the self-awareness that comes from studying the Enneagram. That self-awareness helped me move forward in therapy, disentangle and deepen my personal faith, and connect more authentically with the people I care about.

One of the things I will often say as I coach or teach about the Enneagram is that it's not magic, it's not what will cause change or growth in you. What it is, however, is a tool that can give you self-awareness — and self-awareness must precede any lasting change in our lives. This is the kind of deep self-awareness that awaits you in this book.

Jen P Higgins has found a way to help you uncover the layers that make you who you are. These pages are full of that "simple enough to understand, but deep enough to take you aback" kind of wisdom that brings the complicated, nuanced, often confusing study of the Enneagram into focus where it matters — learning about you.

In true Type 1 Enneagram Coach fashion, I'd like to offer a few words of advice as you prepare to dive into this book:

- **Have a pen and paper handy.** You'll want to jot down the "aha" moments and self-insights that come to mind as you work through the different sections. These notes can offer a lot of clues into those layers and experiences that have built your personality and give you some areas to explore as you put what you learn into practice.

- Speaking of practice, this isn't a book that you read once, find some gold nuggets that give that *dopamine* hit, and never reach for again. Jen will give you tools and strategies — but it's always up to us to take the necessary steps to "unbox" our individual, unique personality. **Take the tools provided and use them!**

- If you have a coach, counselor, therapist, pastor, friend, partner, or any relationship where you feel safe to get vulnerable, please bring up the insights you find out about yourself with them. Having support is so important when we're getting out of our personality comfort zone. Remember that if you don't have this kind of support in your current relationships, there are Enneagram coaches and communities that you can seek out. **You don't have to do this alone.**

And, finally, protect yourself from the self-judgment that so many of us fall into when we start looking under the hood of our personality.

For some, it helps to remind ourselves that what we now see as "flaws" started for a perfectly sensible reason — our coping mechanisms were developed to protect us from real pain or harm early in life. We can grow past those patterns now, without judging or berating ourselves.

For others, it helps to remind ourselves that we are more than our reactions. The parts that make us whole go deeper than the patterns we've put on over time. The patterns we've learned may be cracked and flawed at times, but we aren't.

I truly believe that you will get what you need from this book. Whether you're excited to learn more about yourself, frustrated with your current situation, looking for deeper answers, or all of the above — this book is ready to meet you where you are.

Self-awareness awaits.

Turn the page, friend!

Kim Eddy, author of *The Enneagram For Beginners:
A Christian Guide to Understanding Your Type for a
God-Centered Life*

Introduction

I should have died when I was fifteen years old. I got behind the wheel of a crystal blue Nissan Sentra, which I borrowed from my brother, to drive home from my Saturday morning bowling league. (I promise you I was a cool teenager, despite some nerdy tendencies such as "bowling league.")

It was legal for 15-year-olds to drive large machinery without supervision back then. And being the adventurer that I am and having the car to myself and complete control over the radio station, I took the scenic route along the backcountry roads of rural South Carolina, bebopping to the New Kids on the Block.

The next thing I knew, my face was just a few feet away from a large light pole. The entire hood was shaped like a U and wrapped around the wood just under where the pole was nearly snapped in half. Seeing white steam rising from the engine, I looked to my left and saw a couple running through their front yard towards me. The man opened the door, and I felt the drizzle of rain sprinkle on my face as he asked me questions like "What is your name? Can you move? What day is it?"

This accident was a time before airbags, but after mandatory seatbelts, so fortunately my head avoided the windshield and only hit the steering wheel, but my legs got banged up pretty hard from the crunchy front impact.

My dad was making his rounds at the hospital that morning, and since news travels fast in small country towns, he found out about my accident and came straight to the scene.

I'm not gonna lie… I was kinda hoping my dad would never find out about this little mistake, but he did save me from potentially impersonal care. He examined me at the scene and deemed it safe to move me, and instead of waiting for the ambulance, he carefully helped me into his car and drove me to the hospital himself.

Once home, I remember being in the kitchen all propped up, since climbing stairs was not an option with my black and blue legs, when my mom turned to look at me and said, "You're not supposed to leave this Earth yet."

This was the moment I first understood that my life served a purpose.

Fast forward five years later...

The summer before my senior year of college, the cheerleading squad headed to Myrtle Beach for camp. I had permission to drive myself since that's where I grew up, and I planned to stay with my parents for the week after camp and before classes started.

I saw the squad van pull over ahead of me about an hour into the drive, so I pulled over too, thinking it was a potty break. The coach said, "Guess what, we forgot the uniforms! Since you know how to get to the camp, can you take John back to his dorm and then meet us at camp?"

So, John joined Mark (who was already keeping me company on the 5-hour drive) and me, and we headed back to campus. When we got there, John got the box of uniforms and tossed it in the trunk of my Maxima.

We were chatting when suddenly the car started to shake really badly. We didn't know what was going on, and as soon as I tapped the brakes to disengage the cruise, I started losing control of the car. We hit the embankment, flipped three times, and fortunately the car landed on its wheels, but it caught a little fire.

Actually, the vehicle was consumed in fire and completely destroyed.

We were quickly pulled from the car by an eyewitness who informed me of the blown tire that had caused the accident and the number of loop de loops we made in the air. He called the hospital and sent for an ambulance.

I was in shock sitting on the side of the road watching my car going up in flames. I lost everything I owned in the car (because I was a classic over-packer) with the exception of my day planner (nerd), umbrella, and Bible, all found on the side of the road. (Somehow, they recovered every single uniform, too!)

Aside from a few stitches, bruises, and pinched nerves from the swelling, I walked away from that accident relatively unscathed. John had a mild concussion, and Mark was able to compete at camp the following day.

We were so "lucky" that no one really understood how devastating the story could have turned out until this picture was developed 2 weeks later. Mark's door had been jammed, but he was able to climb out of the window because it was smashed. In the picture, the corner closest to the camera is where John would have been sitting if he hadn't lain down for a nap (with the middle seatbelt on). On either side of the embankment we bounced off, there were steep drop-offs into a wooded valley. And, the very next exit, less than a mile away, was a hospital. So we were able to receive medical attention quickly.

I remember sitting in the ER waiting to get twenty-two stitches in my shoulder and arm and imagining my mom looking back at me saying, "You're not supposed to leave this Earth yet."

I didn't just survive one potentially fatal accident; I had survived two!

I couldn't help wondering if maybe this was a sign that I still wasn't on the right path to my purpose for the last five years. I was getting ready to start my senior year majoring in math only because it was the subject that I got A's in, but it was not my passion.

I was the creepy people-watcher on Ocean Boulevard in Myrtle Beach, South Carolina, where I grew up. People have always fascinated me. The things people do to get attention or to justify their anger. How blind they can be to solutions when they are so close to the problem — when I, an observing bystander, could see the bigger picture, including the simple solutions. I'd want to call out, "Stop yelling at your kid about taking his trash. There's a trash can ten feet in front of you!"

So, I knew pretty early in my life that I wanted to work with people. But already having three medical doctors in my family and not being a fan of chemistry my freshman year of college, I took medical school off the list of possible career paths.

I love helping people be happy and enjoy life. I want everyone to reach the end of their life feeling fully satisfied with how they lived it with no regrets. And there I was, leaving the ER, regretting the academic path I was on that wasn't entirely satisfying me.

I wish I could say that I immediately started following my passion, but honestly, I didn't even know what my passion was. I just knew it wasn't math.

So, per my advisor's suggestion, I took several psychology courses and some business and statistics courses that would help me get into grad school and open up a broader range of opportunities and career paths. At the same time, I could still try to figure out what my niche would be. And that is how I ended up at the business school at the University of Tennessee.

That master's degree landed me a job with the federal government at a corporate university with a team of Industrial-

Organizational psychologists. It was my dream job! I used Statistics and Psychology as we developed our own proprietary personality assessment and evaluation. We used this to boost corporate cultural health, helping employees find value in their work by learning about themselves and aligning their personalities with the company's vision, mission, and core values. How did I get so lucky?

"This was the moment I first understood that my life served a purpose."

As you can imagine, I had to take a lot of personality tests for this project, and this is really where my obsession with personalities began. With every test that I took, I would pour over the report of my test results and devour every new insight I could learn about myself. It was just a piece of paper, but somehow after each test, I felt so heard, seen, and known (sometimes it got a little too vulnerable that I felt naked). That piece of paper helped me not feel so alone in the world.

There's something about personality awareness that unlocks something that's inside of you and liberates a part of yourself that you thought was missing, but it was really there all along. I watched managers and employees we taught and coached through the program understand themselves better. They were more motivated to come to work. They worked harder at their jobs because pride came from a place from inside them. It was not just about "I'm here to get a paycheck so that I can pay another bill." They had a new respect for themselves. They were able to communicate better. They could create better boundaries to help them focus and balance their work life and their home life. Plus, they were able to understand and get along better with their coworkers, which made teamwork a whole lot less stressful and more productive.

Now there were over 13,000 employees at this company. So even though we got great feedback about the project and even received the prestigious Deming Award in 1999 in recognition of our innovative employee development and training initiatives, not all 13,000 employees were transformed or even onboard with "that touchy-feely emotional intelligence hogwash." It was hard for me to watch people reject or make fun of the project. The resistance in some company circles produced the opposite effect. Instead of feeling validated, some employees felt belittled because of their personalities. There were "back-alley rumors" of how our team was just another part of "government control." It all made me wonder if I was really helping people.

So, when the company went through an internal reorganization, I had to make a decision. Do I stay, or do I go? On the one hand, I had job security and made really good money for a twenty-something minority female in Corporate America. At this time (the early 2000s), I had a husband in graduate school and a 6-month-old baby to support. But the personality project was being threatened with termination, and my job would look nothing like the job I fell in love with if I stayed. Plus, this post-partum mama was struggling with being separated from my little guy.

I called my mom for advice. Maybe she would offer more encouragement about my purpose and calling on Earth to help me make this decision. But, this time, it was my dad's words of wisdom that penetrated my soul. I thought, surely he was just going to tell me to suck it up and be an adult. Instead, he said, "Jen, if you're not happy, do something else."

Wait, what?

It's okay for me to quit my job simply because I'm unhappy?

For the record, he didn't advise me to quit my job, but since I was being offered a severance package, I had a built-in deadline to start my own business. I started coaching other work-at-home moms how to align themselves to their businesses. Thus, I continued my purpose of helping people be comfortable and happy being themselves.

I also started teaching clients how to understand personality to build rapport for higher sales, recruiting, and retention. And that's when I saw a pattern. More often than not, I noticed that people were using their personalities as excuses or reasons to not get along with someone else. It permitted them to give up even trying because of personality clashes. I saw it happen in corporate, and here it was happening in the small business space too.

"I'm not asking her because she's an introvert."

"He's so lazy; he must be a Type 9."

"I can't work with her because she is too 'Red.'"

"I just can't do that because I'm not a 'High I' like you are, Jen."

And after a few years, I was weary from the task of trying to break down these barriers and boxes people were putting people in — including themselves.

I thought, what's the point? Default human behavior influences my clients more than my ability to help them break bad habits, stop comparing themselves to others, and swim in their own lanes. It seemed like no matter how hard I tried I couldn't sway the masses. I began to second guess if this was my true calling and questioned who I was to think I could even make a difference here. I found myself in that same position of being unhappy with my career path.

Then, at the age of two, my son Eric began showing signs of autism. He was constantly stimming, ripping paper, throwing shoes, breaking his glasses, biting his brother, and scaring his friends. He was kicked out of three preschools before we realized the root of the issue. He was overstimulated and unable to communicate, and full of anxiety because of that. Once he began getting help for his autism, we discovered that he also struggles with ADHD and Dyslexia.

Through it all, he taught me something more valuable than any of the advice or strategies I learned from his therapy and counseling. Yes, the human instinct of survival is always the stronger influence on behavior. For each meltdown he had, when we could pinpoint this motivation behind his behaviors, we could help him self-regulate.

With that self-regulation, he was calmer to communicate. Because he could communicate, we knew how he needed to be validated, reset, and rebalanced. Learning these strategies helped him get along better with others and create a safe environment for everyone, instead of a chaotic one, walking on eggshells in fear of random triggers. I understood him better; he understood himself better. But we never allowed him to live into his labels. He would never use his diagnosis as a crutch or an excuse that would hold him back but as a guide to how to adjust to get his needs met. He would understand that his circumstances are just different from (but not less than) those of neurotypical people.

When it comes to personality, understanding your perception is different than (but not less than) other people's perceptions is what the Enneagram does so well. It shows us that the default knee jerk reactions we have are borne from a deeply seeded survival instinct to self-protect. Once you know the motivation behind your behaviors, you will be able to self-regulate your responses. Can you imagine what that would do for your self-confidence? Your anxiety? Your relationships? Decision-making in your life and for your business?

Ten years later, when Eric transitioned from homeschooling to a public high school, I prepped him for his Individual Education Plan (IEP) meeting. We met with school staff to set goals and outline accommodations he might need during the school year to support him with those goals. When I mentioned the word "autism," he looked at me in surprise. With his eyebrows raised and his head cocked to one side, he said, "Oh Yeah! I forgot about that. I've just been *being me*."

I've learned three things about *"Being Me"* that I've come to see as universal truths.

1. I have a purpose.
2. I have to be intentional to follow it.
3. I have to be aware of my progress (or lack thereof).

It's the second point that compels me to write this book. Intentionality can be just as elusive as finding your purpose, even when you are 100% certain of who you want to be when you grow up. You can't control your environment. You can't rely on your environment to support your intentions 100% of the time. More importantly, how can you be confident of who you truly are, as opposed to who you were raised or nurtured to be?

In this book, I want to redirect your attention from the nurture of your personality to its nature, the unconscious physiological function of your personality that is lost to your awareness. I'm not discounting the significance of the influences in your life that have shaped who you are today. That's huge! If I had never been in those car accidents, would I be who I am now?

No. I'm taking you back to the time when your brain was so underdeveloped that there was a hole in your skull to allow it to continue growing after you were born. You were entirely dependent on the people in your environment to survive, but only because you were already born with the wiring that allowed you to breathe on your own, pump your own blood, and poop your own poop.

How does the Enneagram help you understand the original wiring of your personality that is still influencing you today?

A study at the University of Edinburgh concluded that "genes play a greater role in forming character traits than was previously thought." Researchers discovered that genes affect a person's "sense of purpose, how well they get on with people, and their ability to continue learning and developing."

I've taken the effort to take complex topics about the Enneagram, Psychology, and Neuroscience and integrate them into an easy-to-follow, story-based narrative. Because each chapter builds on the concepts of the previous chapter, you'll want to read them in order so that you don't miss anything.

> *"Everyone's different and that difference is not a weakness or a label that defines you. That difference is a superpower unique to you that the world NEEDS and the world only benefits from it when you are being true to yourself."*

In Part I, you'll learn about the purpose of your personality and the science behind how your brain processes information from your environment. You'll begin to understand the nature part of your personality as a reflex, a survival instinct, that sets you down a predisposed path.

In Part II, you'll relearn the basics of the Enneagram with a new symbolic perspective, including what it means to *stereotype* and the destructive consequences of *mistyping* yourself and mistyping others. The visuals will help expedite your understanding of each of the nine profiles throughout the book.

In Part III, you'll get to nerd out with me on more brain science as we break down your Enneagram Type into its primitive components, the 9 Acknowledgment Languages™, to better understand what your personality is trying to accomplish on an unconscious level.

In Part IV, you'll learn a simple framework that takes this underlying understanding of your personality's nature to help you self-regulate so that you can stay on track without self-sabotaging your efforts. You'll be able to establish a healthy relationship with yourself first in order to build interdependent relationships with others, so you each get your needs met.

I wish I could tell you that this book will completely unravel the mystery of yourself, but that is an individual path for each person, like Eric's IEP at his school and how I team up with my students and clients as their coach and mentor. However, it will make it easier for you by reframing your behaviors into simple categories to understand and discern for yourself.

You'll know how to acknowledge yourself and get the validation your conscious mind is craving, which will lead to a powerful approach to how you're able to rebalance yourself with healthy boundaries.

This book is a guide to seeing the Enneagram in a new way, not as a "diagnosis" that boxes you in, but as a practical tool and guide for living your life so aligned with who you are that there isn't even a label for it other than you just *Being You*.

That's when you can feel freed up to focus on your own purpose or calling to reach your happiness, fully satisfied with no regrets.

PART I

1

THE REAL PURPOSE BEHIND YOUR PERSONALITY

My sorority sister, Allyson, set me up on a blind date for the Homecoming Dance. He didn't go to our school. She had never met him before; he was a friend of a friend of her date for the dance. She could tell me nothing about him except that his name was Jason and…

"I heard he's got a great personality."

I don't know about you, but isn't that what people tell you when they want you to set your expectations low? But I wanted to go to the dance and enjoy it, so I agreed to take my chances.

The truth is that *personality* explains why we get along instantly with some people and why others are like sandpaper on your face. Simply put, personality is how you behave. But it is so much more than that.

It is shaped by your natural "bent" or *temperament*, your experiences, your habits, attitudes, quirks, and preferences that form your confidences, your insecurities, and most importantly, your character. It is everything that makes you different from anyone else on the planet, just like your thumbprint.

That night, Jason was a great date. He was polite, witty, attractive, and best of all, he laughed at my jokes.

But...

Because most of your personality is unconscious, most of the time you are on auto-pilot (just like the rest of your bodily functions playing in the background). It is not something you can escape. Your personality affects every single thing you do, think, and feel in both small and big ways: from how you take your coffee, to how you buy a car, to how you choose a life partner.

But just like you can temporarily hold your breath or stop blinking, you can also adapt your behavior if the situation calls for it. However, the unconscious part of your personality will shine through with or without your permission. Just like eventually, you'll gasp for air after holding it too long or blink really hard after a staring contest.

So, I had good reason to believe my date was on his "best behavior," and maybe in "real life," he was actually a jerk.

When most people think of personality, they think about a relationship. In fact, the only reason you are aware of personalities is that you noticed differences between two people, usually between yourself and someone else, and generally because your needs aren't being met.

My need to enjoy the dance and have my jokes validated were being met that night. So why was I suspicious of him?

In short, it was a part of my personality. The working definition of personality that I use in my coaching is "a pattern of behaviors you employ to get what you want or avoid what you don't want." In other words, it's strategies to get your needs met.

I had had a bad experience on a blind date in the past where the Prince Charming ended up being Prince Creeper, and I was avoiding a repeat of that experience by being a little too hypervigilant. The irony was that I had forgotten (or thought I had forgotten) that bad experience. Toward the end of the night, Jason asked me, "Are you having a good time?"

"Yeah, I am!"

"Good, I wasn't sure. I was afraid you thought I was a jerk."

That was when I remembered my previous blind date dud, and I realized that it had apparently influenced my behavior. What I thought was me being fun and funny had been experienced as me being aloof and sarcastic.

I was totally self-sabotaging my evening without even knowing it!

Why is it important to understand your personality? To prevent *Experience Gaps* like this one. How I saw myself and how Jason saw me were two different experiences of my personality. How often has this *Experience Gap* happened to you and led to a misunderstanding, an argument, or worse, broken relationships?

If I were to ask you what you would like to get out of studying the *Enneagram*, your answer would probably be "to understand myself better" or "understand other people better," or both — in the hopes that that understanding will improve relationships where both parties are getting their needs met. In other words, you want to get along better with others.

The Enneagram is my favorite personality tool to work with (and I "dated" a lot of personality tools over the years before "marrying" the Enneagram; more on that later). The Enneagram explains the unconscious motivations underneath your patterns of behaviors. And how it can vary depending on your stress level and your ability to make healthy decisions for yourself at any given moment.

You don't have to feel stuck on a path. You can reflect and choose a healthy response, build intentional boundaries, and forge a new path at any time. Like I did in the story I shared in the Introduction of transitioning from majoring in math to getting into business school to landing the psychology job of my dreams. It doesn't have to be a dramatic, overwhelming, 180-degree change overnight and it rarely follows a linear course. As you start to discover why you do what you do, you'll start seeing patterns emerge — patterns that will help you begin to predict your responses and eventually redirect the unhealthy responses to healthy ones.

Amir Levine, the author of *Attached*, says, "Humans are a heterogenous species, varying greatly in appearance, attitudes, and behaviors... if we were identical, then any single environmental change would have the potential to wipe us all out."

Your personality is as unique on the infinite *Personality Spectrum* as a color's wavelength is on the color spectrum. The paint chip displays at your home improvement stores are just a fraction of the actual colors. You know this if you've ever struggled to match the paint on your bathroom wall to patch a hole. Even so, two cans labeled the same color will have variation within a margin of error. Each is unique, even when your eyes can't detect it.

Throughout your life, you've coped, adapted, and survived your environment and formed layers and layers of behavioral patterns. Buried beneath the layers lies the seed of your unique core gift. You bring this gift into the world to serve a higher purpose in your life that no one else can redeem. With the Enneagram, you're not just asking yourself, "Who am I?" but also, "Who am I in the world?"

So why don't more people invest their energy in discovering and understanding how their personality operates?

They are Unaware

If you're like most people, you don't know that your behaviors even have patterns. Nor that when you are stressed, you show different patterns of behaviors than when you feel secure. Perhaps you just think you are inconsistent or "weird" or "crazy" or "broken." You aren't being inconsistent at all. Different stimuli lead to different behaviors.

Later in this book, you'll see you are being remarkably consistent with your personality's reflexes every single time. You just need to understand the purpose or motivation of the behavior. If you don't know what the objective is, everything appears random. It feels impossible to follow or anticipate what will happen next.

When you know the intention behind an action, a different system in your brain is activated, and suddenly, awareness appears. Because your motivations (and not your behaviors) determine your Enneagram Type, it gives you a shortcut to those intentions and awareness.

They are Overwhelmed

You know the priority of understanding what makes you tick and what fills your cup, but the journey is haaaaaarrrrd and takes too loooooooong. You Googled it and find every Enneagram influencer has a different approach. Plus, the sheer volume of information is just... a lot. And, every time you make a breakthrough, it feels like you have to stop and re-experience your life through this new perspective.

Personality is both nature and nurture, but you can only "see" your nurtured personality. You justify character traits that you get "from Dad" or "from your corporate days." And every once in a while, when you can't justify it (or can't invent a meaning), you might say, "Well, that's just who I am," and leave it there, shrouded in mystery. And that mystery can make it a more lengthy and more arduous journey to unravel.

Sigh.

The Enneagram can't answer all of your "nurture" questions about your personality, but it does tackle the "nature" part well.

It describes the hard-wiring of your personality that is written in your DNA. When you were born, your brain was incomplete. Studies show that the brain reaches its peak functioning between twenty and twenty-five years old. During that time, your personality is being nurtured or conditioned by your environment and experiences, such as culture, childhood, and major impactful events or milestones.

The way you experience your environment shapes the skills and values that you develop. For example, my first cousin Carina and I were born exactly 1 week apart. But she was born and raised in the Philippines and taught to be bilingual, a skill I covet. She also eats rice for breakfast, lunch, and dinner — even though she moved to the United States as an adult over two decades ago. I love rice too, but I don't cook 12 cups a day. Those aspects of our personalities were shaped by our nurturing.

Your preferences (or values) and skills (or strengths) are two of the legs on what I call your *Personality Tripod*. I'll go deeper into the metaphor in Part IV for understanding how to keep your tripod balanced and stable. A third leg would be handy for that, which are your motivations.

Paradoxically, your experiences are also shaped by your personality. You have what I call a *Personality Paintbrush* that you use to "paint" the world around you. This is a fancy way of saying you project your own personality's perspective and motivations onto the world. You make innocent (and sometimes not-so-innocent) assumptions about other people or justify why they behave the way they do. You "paint" the mirror you look into as well, meaning you can make assumptions about yourself regarding your own values, strengths, and motivations.

How can you be confident of who you truly are instead of who your environment nurtured you to be?

In his book *Attached*, Levine describes a genetic study at the University of Kansas, where researchers have shown a genetic predisposition to attachment styles. Attachment styles are developed through relationships and therefore are nurtured. In this study, a particular pattern of dopamine receptors was identified to be consistent with those tending to have an anxious attachment in their relationships.

Motivation is triggered in your brain by the neurotransmitter dopamine. Dopamine is the chemical messenger between your nerve cells that tells you when you're being rewarded and punished. Your personality is responsible for the emotional response to that pleasure or pain. Therefore, dopamine also plays a significant role in your ability to think and plan.

Psychologists and pediatricians use the term temperament to describe a person's inborn traits and natural predisposition as it affects their behaviors. These include traits such as biological rhythms, activity level, adaptability, sensitivity, approach/ withdrawal, persistence, distractibility, and mood. According to Mary K Rothbart, PhD, psychologist and author of *Becoming Who We Are*, these traits present prior to developing higher cognitive and social aspects of personality.

Doesn't it make sense, then, to include personality among the biological body systems, like your circulatory, respiratory, or digestive systems that are helping your body function?

That means the real purpose of your personality is... Survival.

Your body is always healing and renewing itself to stay alive and comfortable. Got a papercut? White blood cells are on their way! Old cells die, but they are replaced with new cells. At the slightest imbalance that stresses the body, you have a system of systems working to correct it, to maintain a stable equilibrium or *homeostasis* without you having to lift a finger (unless, of course, that's where the papercut is). Your Health Wellness focuses on optimizing your body's systems to maintain this balance.

As with your personality, old habits die and are replaced with new ones. Your usual coffee brand has been discontinued, and now you use this other brand for your morning coffee (for survival and comfort). Your *Personality Wellness* is a term I coined to describe the part of your health wellness for optimizing your behavioral responses to support the nature of your personality.

The body also has the ability to improve itself. You can form new mind-body connections, even reorganize existing neural connections to improve your body's functions. You can build more muscles to be stronger, increase your lung capacity to hold your breath longer, or train your vocal cords to sing better. This is called *neuroplasticity*, your brain's ability to change and adapt as a result of experience. Likewise, you can improve your mood to increase your survival and comfort and reorganize new thought patterns.

People say things like "Change your Thoughts and Change your Life," meaning change begins with your thoughts. But the truth is, without awareness and purpose, your thoughts will follow your emotions by default. However, as part of your personality, your emotions serve an unconscious physiological function to survive by default. So even when you change your thoughts, your actions will follow the emotions of your personality, which can often seem incongruous to what you believe or have the ability to do.

Many ADHD influencers have learned to embrace and acknowledge how they are wired instead of fighting it, denying it, or ignoring it, and are happier and more successful because of that. "Follow the Dopamine" is a popular slogan for ADHD Awareness to describe the nature of attention dysregulation. With this new awareness, other ADHDers feel more validated and less compelled to compare themselves to neurotypicals.

As you hear in the *Unbox Your Personality* podcast intro, "Stop comparing yourself to others and plug into what is uniquely you... your happiness makes you more effective at bringing out the best in others." Isn't that why you follow the dopamine? Happiness.

But that isn't the failsafe path to the happiness you're looking for. Too much of a good thing is just as threatening to your health wellness and survival as not enough. That's why I say pursuing healthy behaviors unique to your ability is your *Personality Wellness* goal. This pursuit requires understanding the boundaries of your personality's nature and discerning what is healthy for you (which may not be a healthy move for someone else).

In the next chapter, you'll learn about the neuroscience behind how your brain is naturally wired to process information from your experiences, logically and emotionally, and what the unconscious part of your personality is paying attention to.

2

THE BRAIN BEHIND YOUR PERSONALITY

I have a love/hate relationship with water. I love being on the beach, but I don't like swimming in the ocean. I'll jump in the pool, but I don't want to get my hair wet. It's the only beverage I order in restaurants, but I rarely finish my glass because I don't care for the faint taste of chlorination it can have.

Still, water is necessary for survival, so it's not often you'll catch me without my reusable water bottle on me. On average, the human adult body is 60% water. But too much water in the wrong places can cause damage, even death. Edema in your limbs, bad. Fluid around your lungs, bad. Hyponatremia, really bad. Stay hydrated but don't over hydrate, or it can be fatal.

Water by nature takes the path of least resistance, which is why edema is primarily seen in the feet or ankles due to gravity. The same is true for rivers. They all flow downhill. This is also the nature of your personality. The path of least resistance is the dopamine trail. But just like rivers in a rainstorm, having too much dopamine — or too much dopamine concentrated in some areas of the brain and not enough in other areas — can flood you with signals that cause poor impulse control, aggression, and addictive behaviors.

The utility company I worked for was in the "river-taming" business. A network of dams allows for the prevention of floods and erosion by controlling the rivers' flow and for broader social purposes, like recreation and hydroelectric power. The dams provide boundaries to nurture or encourage the water to behave a certain way for the betterment of the community.

An unstable dam is unpredictable — a disaster waiting to happen. That is why there are systems in place to prevent and monitor the effectiveness of the dam. An engineering team regularly rappels or dives along the dam to check for cracks (because water by nature will leak into those cracks, making them bigger until the dam breaks). The flood gates help regulate the water levels after a downpour to prevent flooding. If the dam isn't stable or maintained, the water could do the very opposite of assisting humans by causing death or by washing away homes and crops.

Your personality also has a figurative structure that needs to be intentionally monitored. Like the dam, it respects the nature of your personality but also harnesses the power of your personality to give you something stable to stand on. That's your *Personality Tripod* I mentioned in the last chapter. Each leg is a core trait of your personality you must be aware of that is critical to your *Personality Wellness* or your ability to self-regulate (maintain homeostasis).

Without boundaries and systems that check in and work with the nature of your personality, you could be wasting your energy working against your personality. You spend so much time "avoiding what you don't want" (what your dopamine receptors tell you is a punishment) that you miss the bigger picture goal and undermine yourself.

"Without boundaries and systems that check in and work with the nature of your personality, you could be wasting your energy working against your personality."

What if the dam engineers spent all their time only repairing the cracks visible right at or above the waterline? It would actually compromise the entire dam, making the cracks under the water more vulnerable to the water pressure.

Later in this book, I'll share a simple framework you can apply to your own personality to help you stay balanced and stable to prevent your proverbial drowning of overreacting, overworking, or overthinking that can lead to self-sabotage and be the "death" of you, figuratively, and sadly sometimes literally.

Cracks in the dam under the water are like cracks in the legs of your *Personality Tripod*. If ignored, the structure's integrity will be compromised and could cause it to buckle under its own weight. But because these cracks aren't visible, you might not be aware they are there. Or perhaps you do know they are there but simply forget about them.

How You Forget

Have you ever said any of the following to yourself?

"Why did I walk into this room?"

"Oh, the answer is on the tip of my tongue!"

"I should know better than this! What was I thinking?"

"Wait a minute…I think I've heard this before."

"I don't even know what I want anymore."

"Why do I keep doing the same stupid things over and over again?"

The answer is that you forget! And forgetting is okay. Humans are forgetful creatures. It doesn't mean you didn't learn anything. It just means that once your brain decided it didn't need that information anymore, it wasn't given priority to be remembered.

Can you imagine if you remembered everything that you've ever learned during your entire lifetime? Your brain would melt! Do you really need to be able to recall everyone's favorite color you learned at that "getting to know you" ice breaker in the 5th grade?

Two main characteristics of your forgetting nature can lead to self-sabotage:

You are Simply Unaware

You don't know what you don't know. At least on a conscious level. You don't know things about yourself that you rely on others to point out or mirror back to you, like how Jason thought I was being aloof on our blind date.

Have you ever been in a conversation with a friend over lunch, munching on a salad, when suddenly she stops mid-sentence to tell you that you have spinach in your teeth? That's a good friend, by the way. I've gone all the way to the 5 o'clock hour and commuted back home, just to glimpse in the mirror and see spinach in my teeth. I was totally unaware it was there for the entire afternoon! OMG, who did I talk to, and why didn't they tell me?

My not knowing about the spinach in my teeth didn't change the fact of its existence.

You are Utterly Overwhelmed

You are constantly taking in information from your environment. In a single second, your body has sensed 11,000,000 bits of information for your brain to process, but your *conscious mind* is only able to process fifty bits per second.

Still, processing does not equal remembering. Your short-term memory can only hold about seven, plus or minus two, bits of information at a time. Remember in the 1980s when "area code" actually meant something? You didn't have to dial those three numbers if you were calling within the same area code. You could memorize your friend's phone number she gave you in the hallway because there were only seven digits. As soon as you get to class, you jot it down inside your Trapper Keeper before you forget.

Instead, let's say your friend said, "Call me at home if it's before 8 o'clock, but after that, call me at Michelle's house," and she gives you two sets of phone numbers. You probably won't remember either one of them! That's called *cognitive overload.* This happens when your working memory receives more information than it can handle comfortably, and it compromises your memory and *learning*.

You will also forget information that you never pay attention to. For example, there's a video on YouTube called the "Monkey Business Illusion." In it, they show two teams of kids passing a ball to each other while walking around on a stage. You're meant to count how many times the ball was passed between the team wearing white. The ball is passed slowly at first, and then they start passing the ball much faster. I proudly blurted out "Sixteen!" at the end of the video. I was right, but I totally missed the person in a gorilla suit walking across the stage. It wasn't even a stealth gorilla move. When the video is replayed, you can see the gorilla stop in the center stage and do a little animated chest-beating. In fact, as the gorilla exits, he gets in the way of one of the girls on the white team as she starts to pass the ball to a teammate. She even hesitates and then laughs as she lets the gorilla sidestep her. My brain saw that last bit but didn't encode it as a gorilla. Since I wasn't paying attention to it, I forgot it. Once I knew to look for the gorilla, it was obvious, but I missed other details about the video that I don't want to spoil here. Go look it up.

Your brain is efficient, and if your brain doesn't think you need to know it, you forget it! Why take up brain space for that? Your brain will only learn and hold the capacity for what it needs to survive. Learning depends on your memory. If you can't remember what you sensed, then learning can't occur.

How You Remember

Nothing is more frustrating than starting to tell a joke and then forgetting the punchline.

Your memory fails you because the information didn't make it out of your short-term into your long-term memory. So, you don't even have the memory that you learned the information in the first place. Or you don't have enough clear associations to expedite the process to recall it.

This failure is called retrieval failure, and it can feel like starting over from square one and having to relearn something. Information that doesn't go through the entire processing path from input to long-term memory might not get retrieved or remembered into your consciousness. However, it is still there, and you sometimes just need something to "jog your memory" to recall the information.

And remembering can be so validating! Even if you did ruin the joke with poor comedic timing.

There are two main strategies to help improve your memory and learning: *repetition* and *association*. In psychology, this is called *rehearsal*.

Repetition is when you repeat the coupon code over and over again until you get to the website and can enter it on the checkout page. But this usually only gets stored in your short-term memory, so you'll soon forget it. Therefore, *Spaced repetition* is a better strategy for actual learning. Spaced repetition exposes the same information over again but at longer intervals. Like how you memorized the "Alphabet Song" in kindergarten when you were five years old (and can still sing it from memory today). Each exposure was a reinforcement of the information because it is being rehearsed like "Practice makes Perfect."

Association is when you connect new information to already learned information or memory, like using, "Roy G. Biv" to remember the colors of the rainbow, or saying "This tastes like chicken," "George was the guy in the tropical shirt," or "Mara laughs like my grandmother."

Metaphors, analogies, acronyms, symbols, and images are great mnemonic devices to learn by association: the more *sensory* or emotional the association, the more effective the rehearsal. However, sometimes the association can be completely random or unrelated, like remembering your pin number by its pattern on the keypad or how the Enneagram assigns a number to a set of behavior patterns.

When my son Eric was in the 4th grade, I took him out of the public school system to homeschool him using a dyslexia program. When it was time to teach him fractions, I thought I would pull my hair out. For three years, we tried several different curricula to find a good fit. Let me remind you that I was a math major in college, and I was completely tapped out.

I gave him mnemonics like "D" for the denominator is "D" for down below the line. Finally, I resigned with, "That's good enough. At least he understands decimals."

When he went back to public school for high school, he came home one day and said, "Remember when fractions were hard? Now they're easy." Well, those three years of fractions have been redeemed! He just needed enough spaced repetition and associations to make it stick for him to retrieve it.

So don't get discouraged when you mysteriously find yourself in the same situations, learning the same lessons. It's easy to be hard on yourself and think you are stupid, broken, or incapable. The more repetitions and associations you can make (the more you rehearse something), you increase the likelihood of *retrieval*, or learning from it, later.

Sometimes retrieval failure isn't a failure at all; sometimes it is because higher priority reflexes have taken over. Yes, I'm talking about survival instincts. If you're finding you have been sabotaging your efforts to be happy and successful, then you must shift your focus to a different part of your brain.

Your Three Minds

When you are sitting in a boat on the lakeside of the Norris Lake Dam in Tennessee near where I live, you can only see the bridge and the top twenty feet or so of the dam. The other 90% of the dam is under the lake. This is similar to Sigmund Freud's analogy of an iceberg to explain the three levels of your mind: your conscious, subconscious, and unconscious minds.

The tip of the iceberg that juts out of the water represents your *conscious mind*. You are awake and aware at this level, but you only have access to a surface level of information. These are your thoughts and perceptions in the current moment and rely on emotional and sensory input, even if it is your "mind's eye" imagination. For example, if I don't sense the spinach in my teeth or see it in the mirror, I'm not consciously aware of it. However, if I am afraid or imagine I have spinach in my teeth, I would be self-consciously aware of the possibility and probably check in a mirror.

The *subconscious mind* is just below the surface and holds onto memories and knowledge in storage, but you are not actively aware of them. These are habits and routines that you've learned to do automatically, like cover your mouth when you cough or hold back the passenger next to you when you slam on the brakes — even when no one is sitting in the passenger seat! Your subconscious holds on to the repetitions and associations you've rehearsed, which is also where you jog your memory and are reminded of the things you thought you forgot.

All three minds remember. You don't actually forget; you just lose awareness of the information. If you have sensed it through your body's senses, then your body remembers it. And that information is the largest part of the iceberg and completely submerged underwater. Up to 95% of your brain activity is your *unconscious mind* and taking care of processes in your body that your conscious mind doesn't govern, like your heart beating, eyes blinking, healing, digesting, burping, and so on.

The unconscious mind also includes automatic reflexes that are not learned behaviors, like the Moro or startle reflex in babies, or the patellar reflex, better known as the knee jerk reflex. Reflexes are automatic responses to a stimulus, like a tap under your patella.

You can count on two things when it comes to reflexes:

1. There is always a stimulus that triggers the response.
2. And once the reflex is activated, it must go to completion.

For example, when the doctor loudly claps to test a baby's startle reflex, he expects a few things to happen. He expects the baby to throw his head back and extend his legs and arms, cry out, and then pull his arms and legs back in. Anything different than that exact complete response might indicate that something is not functioning normally.

Sensing incoming information from your environment is also a reflex of your unconscious mind, meaning no one taught it to you, and you didn't create the process (like a habit or routine). To summarize, it goes like this:

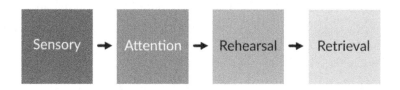

Here's the process, in a nutshell, using big brain words:

New information from your environment first gets picked up by your *thalamus* in your brain. Your thalamus takes in *sensory* information from your eyes, ears, nose, skin, tongue, balance, and position. Then your *amygdala* and *hippocampus* help you decide if you want to pay attention to the information or ignore it. Your amygdala assigns emotional significance to the information (*attention*), and your hippocampus draws a connection between the new information and past information (*rehearsal*) and stores it in your memories. In *retrieval*, during conscious awareness, your *prefrontal cortex* triggers your *executive functioning* and asks, "Do I know what to do? Do I have enough information?" And then, your prefrontal cortex examines all of the relevant memories stored together that can help you make decisions using logic and reason according to your current level of knowledge and awareness.

Whew!

Your executive functioning is how your brain uses what's in your working memory, the flexibility of your common sense or your reasoning skills, and your self-control to help you manage your tasks, emotions, and thoughts.

Here is what I imagine Eric's 9th-grade brain did when he decided that fractions became "easy" for him:

Sensory: His eyes saw the fraction problem on his homework assignment.

Attention: His amygdala processed his fear (possibly of failing, feeling stupid, or getting in trouble if he didn't do his homework) and so paid attention to it.

Rehearsal: His hippocampus connected the problem to the three years of fractions stored in his memory. (association)

Retrieval: His prefrontal cortex logically told him to first calculate a common denominator.

This whole process happens within seconds. And with more rehearsal, the connections will be more robust, and the retrieval will come faster.

If you are familiar with autism or ADHD, you know that people who struggle with these disorders also struggle with executive functioning. So at least for Eric, I can't take the credit for being an awesome math teacher for those three years. It was likely the therapy he underwent to help develop his executive functioning skills that gave him that boost. Through the extra rehearsal in therapy, his brain was able to retrieve the memory stored in his brain from the repetitions during his homeschool.

But something is missing on this information-processing path.

What happens when you are in your *primal self-protection mode* and your survival instincts kick in?

Your Three Needs

Your brain will always prioritize the safety and comfort of your body. This is why you cover your head or run when it starts to rain. Or put on a coat or rub your arms if you get chilled. Your body knows that you need to regulate your temperature or you will get sick.

When you are in *primal self-protection mode*, your body, heart, and mind operate on pure survival instincts and reflexes.

Think of the three primitive *survival needs* of the Animal Kingdom:

Self-Preservation - your body is able, and its functions are safe and in balance (homeostasis). Else, you die.

Social Mate - you are able to attract a mate and procreate. Else, the species dies.

Social Order - you belong and fit into a meaningful role in a hierarchy or structure. Else, you're rejected and left for dead.

Let's look at another simple illustration, starring my younger son, Ryan:

Ryan loves to cook, and he started young. One of my favorite pictures shows him on the countertop on his hands and knees in his Bum Genius diaper, rolling out pizza dough like it is a full-contact sport.

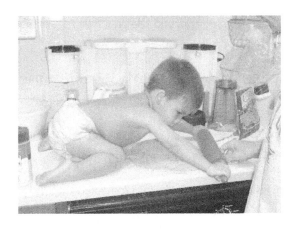

So very early on, he learned not to touch the pot or pan on the stove because it was hot. I would point and say, "STOVE, HOT, OUCH," and he repeated after me in true "Dora the Explorer" form with a firm nod as if to say, "Got it!" And right before every cooking adventure, I would remind him again. "Stove, hot, ouch." And he was careful never to touch the pot.

One day, when he was old enough to be left on his own, I stood back and let him spread his wings. He climbed onto the step stool, and as he leaned over the stove to check the pot's contents, the handle of the pot caught him right at his shirtless chest. He jumped off the stool with a yelp. Once he realized what had happened, he grabbed an ice cube to soothe the burn.

Here is what his brain was probably doing in that split second.

Sensory: His skin touched the pan, and sensory neurons informed him it was hot.

Primal Self-Protection: He jerked away from the hot stove. (Thank you, unconscious survival reflex!)

Attention: His amygdala recognized his fear and paid attention to this hot new sensation.

Rehearsal: His hippocampus connected that the pain on his chest was due to the "STOVE, HOT, OUCH."

Retrieval: His prefrontal cortex told him, logically, that the opposite of hot is cold, and therefore he got an ice cube.

Did you notice that the primal self-protection reflex happens BEFORE the actual information has been processed? And doesn't that make sense? Wouldn't we think something might be wrong with his executive functioning if he stayed there sizzling as he thought about his next move? He was in survival mode, and that reflex took precedence and was perfectly coordinated by his unconscious mind!

"But what does this have to do with personality, Jen?"

The Enneagram explains your unconscious primal self-protection reflexes of your personality, what I refer to as your *Personality Reflex*. This is why when you are constantly in self-protection mode (real or imagined), desperate, and just trying to survive, your primal personality processes take over before your conscious logic does.

You're left wondering why you did what you did, said what you said, or berating yourself that you know better. But just like the knee-jerk reactions, once activated, your *Personality Reflex* must go to completion before the rest of the information can be processed.

Maslow's hierarchy of needs has organized your instinctual needs, often depicted as a pyramid. At the bottom of the pyramid are the foundational needs that prioritize the needs on higher levels. In other words, if you want to meet your self-actualization needs and be your best self, you must first meet your self-esteem needs. But before you can meet those needs, you must fill your need for love and belonging. And if those needs aren't being fulfilled, then the culprit might be because your safety needs or physiological needs are not being met.

These can be simplified into three broader categories that I'll refer to for the rest of this book: *survival, social,* and *self needs.*

When I asked you in the last chapter what would you like to get out of studying the Enneagram, and guessed your answer would be "to understand myself better" or "to understand other people better" in the hopes that both parties would be getting their needs met, I had this image in mind. I am speculating that your focus was more on your social and self needs (to get along better with others) and less on your survival needs.

Did I guess correctly?

Yet, your survival needs are foundational. Humans are the only species in the Animal Kingdom that will ignore their own survival needs for peripheral needs. Still, your unconscious mind always wins.

Despite my suspicions about my blind date Jason, his true personality revealed itself. He was a respectable hard worker at his job, a sensitive mama's boy, and a loyal pen pal even after a year until he met his fiancée and I met my now-husband, Terry (funnily also through a friend of Allyson). It turns out it was me the whole time. My unconscious survival needs for safety and comfort, protecting me from a bad blind date sequel, made the evening awkward.

I'm not making the case here that your survival instincts are always accurate. As in my case with Jason, you can experience a perceived threat as a real one. But more importantly, your survival mode can be activated by a real threat and sometimes backfire. Consider the opossum, infamous for playing dead in the road and inadvertently becoming roadkill. In its natural habitat, that's a handy defense mechanism to ward off predators who prefer live prey. If only the 'possum had the higher cognitive reasoning of humans, he would have assessed the threat with logic and stayed in the brush. Fortunately, you have advanced brains to help you navigate a situation like this more dynamically. And for navigating your *Personality Reflexes*, you have the Enneagram.

Most of the time, the mis-activation of your *Personality Reflex* isn't deadly. The problem with the popular approach to the Enneagram is that when you read about the nine types, you are reading it with your conscious-aware brain and interpreting it as conscious-aware behaviors. When, in fact, the average behaviors of the Enneagram stereotypes describe your primal self-protection reflexes or your survival mode, your automatic knee-jerk reactions, and, oh yeah, by the way, all of that is beyond your conscious awareness.

Once a primal reflex starts, it must continue to completion before moving on to the next stage. This is why it is crucial to examine the natural patterns that the Enneagram teaches. If you can recognize what parts of your personality need to be acknowledged and validated, you're able to know what the red flags are and then choose healthier responses.

Before I tell you how to work with your primal survival needs instead of against them, there are some things you need to know about the Enneagram first.

PART II

3

WHAT YOU NEED TO KNOW ABOUT THE ENNEAGRAM — NOT THE BOX

I didn't always love the Enneagram.

When I was in corporate back in the 1990s, one of my jobs was to help develop a proprietary personality evaluation system as the foundation of fostering and monitoring the company's cultural health. "Emotional Intelligence" and "Play to your Strengths" were the words and phrases buzzing around the office that had my team working like bees on this project.

As a part of this project, I had to take a lot of personality tests. No complaints from me, of course. If you recall my backstory from the Introduction of this book: I was a people-watcher fascinated by behavior. But I had never actually taken a personality assessment before. I didn't even know it was a thing back then.

I suddenly realized, "You know, Jen, you've spent twenty years observing other people, but not a whole lot of time observing yourself!" This was even after those two "life flashing before my eyes" events I described in my backstory!

I discovered the importance of personality for interpersonal skills and that everyone has a different personality.

Aaaand that I really didn't know myself as well as I thought I did! Like, did you know that I'm an extrovert according to one test?

I became obsessed with the results of all of the tests. MBTI, StrengthsFinders, The Big Five, DiSC, to name a few of the big-name assessments that my team researched for the project at work. My obsession bled into my life at home. I started discovering Learning Styles, Spiritual gifts, The 5 Love Languages, His Needs, Her Needs, and all the quizzes I came across in magazines and online. And of course, I made my husband, Terry, take all the tests, too (He's such a good sport.).

It was fun to see myself from these different perspectives and angles, like I had been doing watching others for all of my life.

It was interesting to see the connections between the similar tests, but even more intriguing to see how they were different. Did you know that you can take a test at work and then take the same test at home and get vastly different results? Several times, this happened to me with no real explanation other than "it just depends" on the situation. Like, did you know that at home, I'm an introvert?

My understanding that these situational discrepancies can happen within the same individual is what made me good at working with managers and teams about emotional intelligence and alignment to improve the work culture.

But if I can be candid...

Other than the entertaining collection of data, I personally gained very little from those tests. They didn't change my personal life. They only gave me labels and vocabulary I could use to describe myself.

Unaware and Overwhelmed

For the first seven years of our marriage, my husband Terry and I were a "Dual Income, No Kids" household (D.I.N.K.). Even though we got some pressure from the Filipino side of the family, who were worried that we could not conceive, we stood proud in our D.I.N.K. status, enjoying our freedom to travel for work, travel for fun, and basically do and have whatever we wanted.

The truth was, I wasn't ready to be responsible for little humans. Being the youngest sibling in my home, I didn't have much hands-on experience with babies or children other than observations. Instead, Terry and I had adopted three high-maintenance ferrets, and although they were cute, they were a huge pain in the rear to take care of. This only solidified what I already suspected – I didn't believe I was meant to be a parent.

I was too naïve, too much of an "individualist" (a label a personality test gave me), too self-focused, and I had anger management issues, which I definitely didn't want to pass on to posterity. I had some maturing to do and was grateful to have a faithful husband that was on the same page and was willing to put up with my silly shenanigans and underlying insecurities.

Soon after my husband's 30th birthday, we signed up for a marriage retreat. Each afternoon we were given conversation topics to talk about as homework. One evening, we were discussing expectations versus reality, and he looked at me and casually said, "You know, I thought I'd be a dad before I turned thirty." Clearly, we had some communication issues. We were coming due for the seven-year-itch, but parenthood wasn't what I thought we would be scratching! This is a prime example of me using my *Personality Paintbrush* to make assumptions about Terry and I being on the same page.

After the retreat, we decided to start a family, and I felt an entire energetic shift happen in my soul. Suddenly, I didn't just want to be a parent; I wanted to be an amazing parent! I wanted to be the best role model, and I knew that meant being the best me I could be, including a better wife, daughter, sister, and friend.

Imagine my surprise when we got pregnant right away! Terry was glowing; I was glowing. I had recently gotten a promotion at work, and we just bought our "dream" house. I invested well, ate well, and even started running races with Terry to stay strong and build my endurance. I was so excited about how everything seemed to be lining up. I could see us growing into this house and making it a home, happy and healthy.

Then one Friday, that energetic shift in my soul re-shifted back after a restroom break at an offsite work event when I discovered I was bleeding. Thank goodness I rode with a coworker who willingly drove me the hour it took to go straight to the hospital. That weekend, Terry and I were forced to make alternative plans. Maybe I was right before; perhaps I really wasn't meant to be a parent.

You already know by now that that wasn't true. Still, my soul didn't entirely shift back to where it was before. For some reason, the indulgent lifestyle I led earlier was no longer attractive. What was the purpose of hedonism? I needed to dive deep into my soul and ask myself (yet again): "Who am I?" and "Why am I really still here?"

Aware but Still Overwhelmed

Motherhood. I didn't think I wanted it, but then it was all I wanted.

After our Eric was born, everything shifted once again. I was ready to quit my corporate job to be a full-time mom. Just kidding. That lasted about two months before I got bored. But I was prepared to be a work-at-home mom, to be present in his life, and to fully commit to being the role model he could look up to and emulate.

I built a new business helping other work-at-home moms balance their life by understanding their personalities better, so they didn't have to choose between their kids and their businesses. What a perfect fit for me! It did so well that Terry was able to quit his traveling job. He had gone back to grad school and then landed a desk job that kept him close to me and the kids (Yep, our son Ryan snuck in there, too!).

I loved finally having all four of us together in the home. But it came with its challenges. I needed Terry to be more accessible, especially after Eric's autism diagnosis and having a newborn, but it really made my roles blurry. I was a full-time mom, boss, teacher, meltdown-handler, and basket case. Not necessarily in that order. How was I going to fit in being a full-time wife? I decided to hire an assistant for my business and welcomed an au pair from Brazil into our home for the kids. That way I could keep my business and marriage (and sanity) running.

Wow! That was a lot of transitions! Remember the personality tests that told me my personality "depends" on the situation? Well, I had a lot of situations going on. I'm not gonna lie. I was a hot mess...even if I was the picture of success on the outside. I started to self-sabotage my health, business, and relationships. But I had no idea it was because of my own *primal self-protection mode.*

My purpose was finally clear, but I was depressed. I watched everything I worked hard to create and maintain start to crumble before me. Intellectually, I recognized that I still didn't understand myself as much as I thought I should. Emotionally, I just didn't have the capacity to control my triggers. The worst part, my business was built on helping other work-at-home moms balance their life, and I needed that balance myself.

The Cobbler has no shoes, y'all.

I became one of those people who use personality as excuses or reasons to NOT get along with someone else. I permitted myself to give up on people because we were in different boxes that were not compatible. I had seen this happen in the corporate world and the small businesses of my clients. I was already weary of trying to sway the masses to stop putting themselves and others in a box, and now I had become one of them.

I began to second guess if this was really my true calling, and I was seriously considering scrapping the whole personality thing. If I can't figure this out about myself, then how the heck am I going to help others? Maybe I was doomed to my personality after all… and I couldn't in good conscience continue to teach my clients otherwise.

I didn't know it at the time, but my *Personality Tripod* was crashing down!

That's when I met the Enneagram.

Personal Roadmap for Growth: The Box and The Ladder

Like a spurned lover, I was a little jaded at first because after taking four tests and getting four different results, I was like, "Oof, it's one of those tests."

So, no, it was not love-at-first-sight like its predecessors. But being the personality nerd I am, curiosity got the best of me, so I did my due diligence and studied it anyway. Google, podcasts, Instagram, books, and blogs became my playground.

The more I learned, the more "seen" I felt (Even though I was mistyped at the time! More on that later.). A single type's profile explained why sometimes I needed to be around people, and other times even small doses of people were too "peopley." Sometimes I was the Rockstar, and sometimes I was the Wallflower.

"You mean I just have to understand one type really, really well
  to understand myself really, really well?"

"...And it'll give me a roadmap and show me exactly where I need to go to reach my destination?"

"...And tell me if I'm headed for a dead-end?"

"...And show me the detour route?"

I don't mean to sound lazy or anything, but I needed something that comprehensive in my life to hold my hand and get me out of my funk. So, that's when my "crush" began.

"It gets me... for better and for worse," I mused.

The Enneagram is the only tool that I've found that automatically and intuitively distinguishes the differences between how you behave in stress vs. health. Your Enneagram Type gives you clues about the status of your *Personality Wellness*, like a litmus test, to tell you if you're in the metaphorical box or not. But more importantly, your 'box" comes with a built-in ladder that helps you climb out when you are stuck.

And that ladder is exclusive to YOU!

"If you retain nothing else from this book, please understand that you are NOT the box. You are just in it."

But I must make an important distinction here. Your Enneagram Type isn't you. You are not your Enneagram Type. The Enneagram simply organizes the infinite *Personality Spectrum* into nine categories.

If you retain nothing else from this book, please understand that you are NOT the box. You are just in it. The Enneagram number is the box, not you. When you don't feel seen for who you truly are, you can be misguided and get stuck in your Enneagram box, trying so hard to justify why you do what you do. But if you believe you are the box, then you can't get out of it!

Likewise, if you are already adamant that you will not be put into a box, here's your reality check. You're already in a box, limited by your body's wiring, your environment, and your perceptions. And before you can climb out of it, you must first acknowledge the box. That box isn't you, but it is yours.

The Enneagram allows us to see how we are all the same and how we are all different. We are all human, but we each look different. We all have fingerprints, but they are all different (even from our left hand vs. right). We all have a brain that uses the same process, but we process different experiences based on our different motivations, strengths, and values.

There will be no more keeping up with the Joneses. You have a personal path to guide you and help you establish accurate boundaries — not the boundaries that trap you in your "box," but the boundaries that actually give you the freedom to wholly and unapologetically be yourself.

These lightbulb concepts convinced me that I needed to keep my business open and save my clients from that frustrating waste of time and energy. I started opening up to the idea of switching from the primary personality tool I had been using in my business to the Enneagram instead. So, I started researching how I could "make it official." I immediately enrolled in a 5-week program to get certified as an Enneagram Coach.

To follow through with the cheesy dating storyline, I was now officially engaged to the Enneagram! But stay tuned for the cold feet.

4

WHAT YOU NEED TO KNOW ABOUT SYMBOLS — THE LANGUAGE OF YOUR SUBCONSCIOUS

When my sister graduated from medical school, she planned a European backpacking trip and invited me to join her, just us sisters. Our favorite stop was Greece. We were just preparing to be there for a day, but we loved it so much we stayed two extra days.

Being a mathematician and in a sorority, I was used to seeing Greek symbols on panhellenic paraphernalia or formulas and equations in my textbooks. I was not used to actually reading them to try to form words out of their alphabet. To see the Greek word ναι and not initially pronounce it "vie" instead of "neh" took a bit of effort. The following semester, the nerd in me signed up for Greek as a foreign language. After that class, I had difficulty seeing εγ in a math equation without reading it as "eg." The symbols had now been given a dual meaning in my mind.

When you first discovered the Enneagram, you might have thought, "It's all Greek to me." It can be intimidating to be stuck in the middle of Athens with a map written with the English alphabet, looking at street signs written in Greek (ναι, I got lost trying to find the Acropolis!). Similarly, the jargon, numerology, and symbols of the Enneagram might have been confusing, creepy, or perhaps a little too woo-woo for your taste. But really all you need is a translator, and that is what this chapter will be for you.

If you really want to simplify the Enneagram, the symbol is the most important image to imprint into your subconscious, where the real learning resides in your brain. Images and emotions are the fastest associations for getting this new information from your short-term to your long-term memory.

But the Enneagram symbol is not just a symbol. It's a schematic diagram of the paths your personality takes. It always gives you the bigger picture of your choices on your personal growth roadmap. It's so brilliant; I wish I had invented it myself.

One of the first questions I was taught to handle is "Who invented the Enneagram?" because you'll get different answers if you Google it. And there is a bit of a controversy about it too. In actuality, the Enneagram's origins are unknown, but the system has been observed and used for centuries among scholars and spiritual leaders. Since the system is based on behavioral patterns and motivational categories, no single person can be credited for inventing it. Although the Bolivian philosopher, Oscar Ichazo, was the first to coin the phrase "Enneagram of Personality," the seed of the modern-day Enneagram, he had been denied legal rights to copyright it.

Think of it like this: If you are an ornithologist (a bird scientist) and you're observing a species of birds in the sky. Every day you record what you observe. As you collect data, you notice patterns and how some birds follow a flight pattern differently from other birds in the flock. Then you tell a friend or two, teach it at a university, write a publication about it, maybe start a blog or podcast, and write lots of books explaining and summarizing the flight patterns of these birds for others also to know. Did you just invent the flight patterns of the birds? No, they were already there. You were simply the observer of it. And then the teacher of it, passing on your observations to other people.

This is how you must also view the origin of the Enneagram. Centuries of observers of human behavior patterns worldwide passed on their knowledge from one generation to the next until Oscar Ichazo began teaching his self-development programs in the 1950s, associating the word enneagram with personality. Russian philosopher, G.I. Gurdjieff, is credited with publicly making the popular Enneagram diagram known, but he does not claim to be the actual source. This is the diagram you recognize today that represents the Enneagram of Personality.

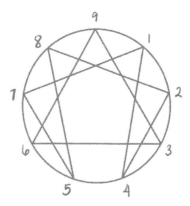

Ennea is Greek for "nine," and *gram* is Greek for a "drawing or diagram." So the word Enneagram quite literally means "a diagram of nine." The diagram of the Enneagram of Personality, now simply known as the Enneagram, has three symbols:

- the numerals 1-9,

- the connecting lines that form a star-like shape,

- and a circle.

The numerals are evenly spaced around a circle like a clock, except this clock only goes to nine instead of twelve numbers. Inside the circle, the nine-pointed shape touches the circle's perimeter at exactly nine points where the numerals are located.

Remember that the Enneagram organizes the infinite *Personality Spectrum* into nine categories. Each numeral represents a broad personality profile or Enneagram Type, sometimes referred to as your Enneagram Number or your *Core Type*.

When I'm teaching this on a whiteboard, I usually draw eyeballs in the middle of the diagram, just as a reminder that the Enneagram represents nine different world perspectives. It's nine different ways to filter the world and how we are wired or motivated to express ourselves through that filter. Later, I'll go through how this corresponds to the automatic process your brain goes through that serves to self-protect (and can sometimes self-sabotage).

You should know a couple of things about the diagram before we move on so that you have a visual image in your mind as you assimilate the rest of the information in this book.

First, the equally spaced intervals between *numbers* around the circle indicate that each Core Type is equally valid. No type is better or worse than another type, but every type has its weaknesses and strengths. You don't get bragging rights for being type #1; you only get bragging rights for expressing the healthy behaviors of your own type. (And, by the way, be sure to celebrate those moments!)

Second, the *lines* connecting the numbers in that star-like shape are actually arrows, and they represent how your personality is dynamic and constantly changing. Each number rests at the base of two arrows. One arrow is the path you take in stress, and the other is the path you take in security. So, in stress, you tend to take on the stereotypical characteristics of the numbers on your *Stress Path*, and when you're feeling secure, you tend to take on those on your *Security Path*. Later, you'll see how this can play a role in you being mistyped in Chapter 6.

"The whole Enneagram diagram represents a microcosm of you and your personality and the macrocosm of the systemic relationships in your environment and the world."

And third, the *circle* represents a cycle, completeness, and wholeness, without a beginning or end. The circle reminds you that you are already valid. You are already complete. What you think is missing is just a blind spot. It is never too late to start your personal growth journey to open your eyes to those spots on the diagram.

But most importantly, the circle and lines connect all of the numbers in a whole dynamic community, which is, in my opinion, the ultimate purpose of the Enneagram.

The whole Enneagram diagram represents a microcosm of you and your personality and the macrocosm of the systemic relationships in your environment and the world. This is how I hope you will see the diagram from now on. Remember, you're not just asking yourself, "Who am I?" but also, "Who am I in the world?" You're not supposed to be tucked away in one corner, operating as a single stereotype.

Everyone is different, and everyone belongs.

"Jen, what symbols does the Enneagram provide to illustrate my unique personality?"

Well, it doesn't. But never fear. Here's another reason why my students love my classes so much. Enter: the LEGO® bricks I borrowed from my kids that they'll likely never get back. That's how popular and effective this imagery has been. I built a small white and gray box with a lid. When you open the lid, inside is a LEGO® extension ladder and a LEGO® mini-figure (It's Emmett for you LEGO® Movie fans). The box itself represents the box of your Enneagram Type, and the ladder represents the

Personal Growth roadmap for that particular type for getting out of your box.

Inside of that box is another symbol, and this is what really makes you unique. It's an image of a three-legged stool that I call your *Personality Tripod* (because personality three-legged stool is awkward to say). One leg represents your motivations, another your strengths, and the third, your values.

You need each of these legs to be able to hold you up when you stand on the stool. It only takes one of those legs to weaken or break to jeopardize its stability. So your goal is to keep the legs balanced and strong or reinforced. That's your *Personality Wellness* goal.

The legs of your *Personality Tripod* include your conscious, subconscious, and unconscious minds. However, because in this book we are focusing on your survival needs, in the image below, I'm strictly referring to your unconscious mind by using the term core to describe your *core motivations, core strengths,* and *core values* of your unconscious mind.

Your core motivations are your strong unconscious desires and fears that trigger your *Personality Reflexes.* These core motivations determine your Enneagram Type.

Your core strengths are your superpowers or the hard-wired abilities your personality offers you. However, when you are overcompensating, they become fixations that can unconsciously thwart your efforts. I'll share some common fixations associated with your Enneagram Type later.

Your core values are what you strongly believe in or value. Even though the Enneagram helps explain why you are drawn more to certain ideas than others, this category is too diverse to responsibly make a general point in a book. Besides, the widespread common use of the term "core values" is more influenced by your experiences or the nurture of your personality rather than nature and is best explored on a person-by-person basis.

"How do all the symbols fit together, Jen?"

I'm glad you asked because fitting them all together will help it stick in your memory. The kookier, the better.

You have your own box that is associated with your Enneagram Type. You're the only one in that box. Even if we are both Type 7, you and I would still each have our own box. Sometimes the lid is open, and sometimes it is closed. Sometimes you are climbing up the ladder, and sometimes you are sliding down (or falling off) the ladder, depending on your level of awareness. You'll see me refer to it as the *Ladder of Awareness*. Sometimes your box moves around the diagram to other numbers' positions as your behaviors change or adapt to your environment. More on that later in Chapter 11.

At the very bottom of your box is your *Personality Tripod*, grounding your personality and supporting your ladder. When your tripod isn't balanced, your ladder isn't stable. Doesn't it make sense to spend your energy learning how to stabilize your tripod? How scary is it to climb a ladder that isn't on solid ground? You'd be even less likely to feel confident enough to extend the ladder above the box.

> *"This 'unboxing' imagery will revolutionize the way you use the Enneagram in your life from now on!"*

Here is the best part! Since I believe finding your role in the community with others is the ultimate purpose of studying your personality, I love the symbolism shown here: each person with their own box connected by the Enneagram. When your tripod is stable, your box lid is open, and you are at the top of your ladder, you can clearly see where you belong in the tribe. And since you are not hiding, others can see and acknowledge you, too.

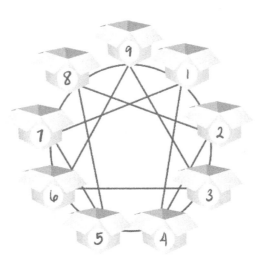

Hold onto these images in your mind for an extra second before you read on. Humans think in images, which allows us to create a "story" that we can retrieve from memory. This is a common tactic taught to memorize so many digits of the number π or the names of the people you meet at a networking event. You can easily envision the whole story, the bigger picture, before making decisions so they are working with your personality patterns. This "unboxing" imagery will revolutionize the way you use the Enneagram in your life from now on! In the next chapter, you will learn about typing yourself or figuring out which Enneagram Type box is yours.

But before we move on, there is one final word about symbols that I must address — *stereotype.*

Did you just cringe?

I used to be that way too. Every meme that would typecast other people's behaviors would make me laugh until I realized that it was rude and that those behaviors could be any Enneagram Type depending on their "nurture." A stereotype is a widely held but fixed oversimplification of a person or thing and can feel so boxing. It's like judging every used-car salesman as pushy or sleazy. Yet, I've never had a car buying experience like that, so it isn't fair to assign that label to all used-car salesmen.

The word *stereotype* is Greek for "solid form." In the 18th century, printing publications on paper was painstakingly slow. It was a movable type, meaning every single individual letter needed to be perfectly aligned to form the words, sentences, and paragraphs on a single page. After hours of putting it together, it got inked and pressed onto paper X number of times, and then all the individual letters were cleared off to do it again for the next page. So to speed up the process and keep up with printing demands, a stereotype was created. It was a "solid form" made from the impression of one of those moveable type pages and used to print multiple identical copies on rolls of paper on the printing press. Over time, the word's meaning shifted to describing people or ideas as the "expected impression from a stereotype."

For the longest time, I was totally against Enneagram stereotyping. Whenever I caught even the slightest hint that someone might be misjudging what it means to be a Type 5, I would throw "look-alike" types into the mix or other attempts to open their mind about the possibilities of how a Type 5 might "look." I eventually realized that I was confusing people who were trying to type themselves. I was doing them a disservice by keeping them stuck in *Typing Mode*. They really needed a set of common behaviors that were more of the rule than the exception.

When you tell a friend that your kid is going through the "terrible twos," they can make assumptions about her behavior without you having to go into detail. They aren't making a judgment about you or your daughter. It is simply a tool to make communication easier. Assumptions are neutral; judgments hurt.

So, I changed my tune a little and loosened my collar a bit once I recognized that a stereotype is just a tool that symbolizes the expected impression of an Enneagram Type that makes finding your type more accessible and faster. So, I use the word stereotype, not as a judgment, but as a symbol describing the "average behaviors" of a type, which helps to distinguish the types better.

I'm no longer against using stereotypes. Rather, I'm really against the caricatures of Enneagram Types that exaggerate the behaviors with a cynical or satirical mindset. This can create a larger *Experience Gap* that is harder to close and can lead to boxing, misunderstandings, and broken relationships.

Then, the goal is not to stop stereotyping the numbers, but to stop wrongfully stereotyping them. This can be hurtful and, worse, lead to mistyping. In the next chapter, you'll read about how to avoid this by learning the rules for typing and each type's stereotypical motivations and mindsets.

5

WHAT YOU NEED TO KNOW ABOUT (MIS)TYPING YOURSELF

On the very first day of class to train for my Enneagram certification, I introduced myself and happily announced that I was not a newbie to the Enneagram. On a scale of 1-10, where one is "brand new" and ten is "Ninja Master," my self-reported score was an impressive 7.5 because I had had over a year of studying under my belt. This wasn't my first rodeo, you know.

I also confidently shared with the class that I was a Type 4 because I am an "Individualist." (Spoiler alert: I'm not a Type 4, but I was very good at justifying myself as a Type 4). And for the first few weeks of the program, I was the "resident" Type 4 of the class, always giving appropriate Type 4 answers to all of the Type 4 questions.

This just shows you can know a lot about the Enneagram and still not know anything about the Enneagram.

In the very last week of my training, I had an epiphany! While multitasking, I listened to this well-produced documentary-style audiobook about World War II. There were live interviews with veterans and survivors of the war. I knew the Hiroshima part of the story was coming up, and I had expected I'd be very emotional and upset listening to realistic sound effects and the original broadcast coverage. So I went back to my bedroom to brace myself and had my Kleenex ready to sop up all of my tears.

But that didn't happen. I didn't shed one tear. However, my stomach was in knots with anxiety anticipating how it would sound and how I would react.

I realized at that moment, based on the training and coaching I had received in the certification program, there is no way I could be a Type 4. (Listen to episode 20 of the podcast for the whole story.)

Then I got mad (still working on that anger management…).

"Well, then… which type am I?" I said to no one in the room. "Did I just completely waste my time (and money) studying a bogus system? Does this mean I've gotta start ALL OVER?"

I started to get cold feet about marrying the Enneagram the following week when my training was ending. I let out a deep sigh and looked over at the Best Man (Terry) and broke the news to him that there may not be wedded bliss with the Enneagram.

"You've got one more week. Send a message to your mentor and get some coaching," he suggested. (Thanks, Terry, for grounding me!)

Finding your type by yourself is complex because your Enneagram Type is determined by a unique set of core motivations that are primal, default, knee-jerk, unconscious triggers embedded in your psyche.

Even after all the studying I did before the program, I still needed coaching on top of the twenty hours of certification-level training in order to feel 100% confident of my Enneagram Type! Turns out… I'm actually a Type 7 and am still baffled to this day about how confident I was that I was a Type 4 when it is so clear to me now why I'm not.

Cognitive bias is a fickle punk. Like your *Personality Paintbrush*, it affects how you view and interpret the world around you. It's the tendency to pay attention to new information that favors your own ideas and how you mold new data to confirm your own existing beliefs or theories.

This is kind of an embarrassing story because when I was soooo sure that I was a Type 4, I was spreading a lot of misinformation during coaching sessions with clients, coffee chats with my friends, and the people in the group that were training to become Enneagram coaches!

Oops.

But I know I'm not the only one guilty of this. I'm not even the only one aware that I'm guilty of this. And there are more people out there guilty of this and they don't even know it! Clients who came to me thinking they were a specific Enneagram Type often left the session identifying themselves as a different type!

> *"Finding your type by yourself is complex because your Enneagram Type is determined by a unique set of core motivations that are primal, default, knee-jerk, unconscious triggers embedded in your psyche."*

"Confidence is comforting. The lure of certainty is built into the brain at a very basic level," says Jonah Lehrer in his book, *How We Decide.* But we must be patient and humble that we are not overconfident and risk mistyping. The worst consequence of being mistyped is being on the wrong Personal Growth roadmap. My mistyping explained why I wasn't seeing the growth results you'd expect following Type 4's roadmap. I had more to unbox!

Typing yourself alone is the hard road. But if you like a challenge and have some extra time on your hands, it's not impossible. View it as an elimination process using the rules below.

Enneagram Typing Rules

Rule #1: Your Core Type is determined by your MOTIVATIONS, not your behaviors.

Rule #2: You only have ONE Enneagram Type, and it never changes.

Rule #3: Use the NUMBERS, not the archetypal labels, to avoid wrongfully stereotyping.

These are the three Typing Rules that every person should know about the Enneagram to reduce your chances of being mistyped.

These rules will put a stone in your shoe and challenge your *cognitive biases* when you start to gravitate to only one type and are tempted to abandon your elimination process. Boy, I sure wish someone had told me about these 3 simple rules all of those months that I thought I was a Type 4!

If you don't know your Enneagram Type yet, by the end of this book, you should have a pretty good idea or at least have it confidently narrowed down to two or three types. Write these rules down on a sticky note to reference while you're in Typing Mode so that you don't lose sight of them. When these rules are broken, they often lead to mistyping.

Motivations, Strengths, and Mindsets of the 9 Enneagram (stereo)Types

Below is a scandalously brief introduction to the nine stereotypes of the Enneagram. It might feel like an exceptionally formulaic system to squeeze the infinite number of personalities of the *Personality Spectrum* into a list of just nine profiles. And it is. That's why viewing your personality only at this level is NOT or EVER an accurate way to type yourself.

I am only highlighting each type's core motivations and average stereotypical behaviors in the spirit of not overcomplicating things. I also include a core strength and mindset for each type. In Part III of this book, we'll explore the types deeper at the unconscious "nature" perspective when you learn about the 9 Acknowledgment Languages™.

Type 8's want to be strong, so they are aggressive and strong-willed but fear being controlled. They have a natural strength of "willpower." And they have a mindset to "overpower."

Type 9's want to be at ease, so they are "chill" and self-effacing but fear being disconnected. They have a natural ability to bring "harmony" or "togetherness." And they have a mindset of "inertia."

Type 1's want to be proper, so they are principled and idealistic but fear being corrupted. They have a natural strength of "integrity." And they have a mindset of "restraint."

Type 2's want to be appreciated, so they are generous and seductive but fear being seen as needy. They have a natural ability to "nurture." And they have a mindset of "flattery."

Type 3's want to be admired, so they are ambitious and status-conscious but fear being seen as an imposter. They have a natural strength for "self-assurance." And they have a mindset to "compete."

Type 4's want to be different, so they are mysterious and emotionally authentic but fear not being seen as original. They have a natural ability to "endure." And they have a mindset of "melancholy."

Type 5's want to be factual, so they observe and collect data but fear being depleted. They have the natural strength of "honesty." And they have a mindset to "detach."

Type 6's want to be supported, so they advocate and make systems but fear being unprepared. They have a natural strength of "dependability." And they have a mindset of "doubt."

Type 7's want to be content, so they are indulgent and optimistic but fear being deprived. They have a natural ability for "immersion." And they have a mindset to "explore."

Again, these alone are NOT sufficient descriptions to use for typing yourself (and especially not others!).

You probably see yourself in more than one description. That's normal because, as part of the human species, you have the capacity to want, fear, do, and think all nine of them. And the more self-aware you become, you'll be able to access these different parts of yourself more easily so you can better connect with people of other Enneagram Types.

The description representing the nature of your personality will be your core Enneagram Type, the one you were born with and still have, regardless of how much you have matured or adapted your behaviors to your environment.

Using the symbols, your Core Type is the part of your *Personality Tripod* at the bottom of your box that grounds your ladder. This is the unconscious nature of your personality that you are trying to balance. In contrast, it's your nurturing and environment that explain your most immediate conscious-aware behaviors.

The Causes and Consequences of Getting Your Type Wrong

With the popularization of the Enneagram, it seems like everyone has heard of it. And the quickest way to feel like you're "in the loop" is to Google it.

Oh, look! A free online quiz… click. And twenty minutes later, the test results tell you "You're an Achiever!" with the same amount of accuracy as "You're a Gryffindor!" on the Harry

Potter quiz you took on Facebook. You know, the one that has a button that says, "If you don't like your results, click here and try again."

Let's say you took it more seriously and invested money in a reputable assessment, and you took the time to really reflect and think about your answers. You might still be mistyped.

Dennis was asked to take an Enneagram assessment when hired at a company. Not only was there a questionnaire, but there was also a live interview as part of the assessment. I commended the company for its due diligence to take the questionnaire results with a grain of salt and take a *narrative approach* to typing by having an actual conversation with Dennis. The results were in, and he was told he was a Type 3. On the outside, Dennis's behaviors were consistent with a Type 3. He's charming, ambitious, and had a laundry list of impressive achievements, and he was barely thirty years old.

As I got to know Dennis, he would unconsciously make comments like "not for the weak" or "mind over matter" that gave me pause to ask him, "What other numbers do you think you might be if you weren't a Type 3?" And like most people, he had no idea. He had only learned about Type 3 because that's all the report gave him. After coaching him through a process of elimination and a week or two of reflection, he recognized that his ability to achieve was a more significant focus than his actual achievements. "Failure is not an option" was his motto, not because of a scoreboard or a fear of being "found out" that he wasn't as great as his resume touted, but rather because failing meant he wasn't able to succeed or not strong enough to carry out the goal. Exploring his behavior patterns on these Stress and Security Paths verified that his Core Type is an Eight.

Remember the lines on the diagram? And how each type has one line representing its Stress Path and one line representing its Security Path? As a Type 4 "poser," my Security Path would take me to Type 1, meaning if I am behaving like a stereotypical Type 1, then I am on my Security Path, or sometimes the *Growth Path*. This is called *Integration*.

Yay, me!

But — and it's a big but — as a Type 7, the Type 1 stereotypical behaviors are a red flag that I've traveled down my Stress Path. That's *Disintegration*.

Oops, again.

Because I was mistyped, I duped myself into thinking I was on the "healthy" track to my personal development when I was actually going in the opposite direction, entirely unawares. I definitely don't want anyone to make this kind of mistake. Why make a long journey longer?

"Soooo, Jen… is there a shortcut?"

Has there ever been a shortcut to personal growth? No, but if you're asking me if there is a shortcut to finding your Enneagram Type, then yes! And it is not by taking a test.

In the next chapter, you'll learn the best way to discover or confirm your type through a process of elimination and using the Typing Rules. Got that sticky note handy?

6

WHAT YOU NEED TO KNOW ABOUT ENNEAGRAM ASSESSMENTS

The fastest way to discover your Enneagram Type is to find a qualified Enneagram coach who uses the narrative approach. This approach isn't an interview-like typing session that can feel like an interrogation, but rather, it's a conversation with a purpose. When your coach asks you the right questions, and you share your story, your true type will reveal itself through the patterns they are trained to observe because they understand the infrastructure of the Enneagram. An experienced Enneagram coach can often recognize nurtured layers that mask your true Core Type and consider your energy and body language as part of your typing session that you can't get from a test.

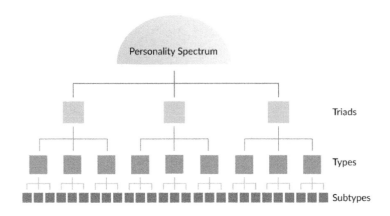

Your coach will be trained to recognize and discern a hierarchy of concepts: *Triads* are at the top level of the chain, then *Types* below that, and then *Subtypes* at the lower level.

While most people who are dabbling in the Enneagram only focus on Types and Subtypes, qualified Enneagram coaches focus on the characteristics of the Types at the Triad level and start the process of elimination from the top.

Most Enneagram books and teachers will talk about your three *Centers of Intelligence*: thinking, feeling, and moving, so I was familiar with the concepts before my training. But it wasn't until I got the certification training that I understood just how crucial the Centers of Intelligence are to the typing process. Over time

I learned about other sets of triadic groups of the Enneagram Types. More on this in Chapter 7, as this is the basis of the 9 Acknowledgment Languages™.

If you compare notes with someone who isn't a qualified coach, you will still benefit from having their objective view to help overcome biased pitfalls and other blind spots that can interfere with typing yourself. But don't be swayed by fanatics who quickly type themselves through books and tests or try to tell you what type they think you are. You're the YOU expert.

Remember, most people don't get it right the first time, so you might not either.

Here are some facts that made me feel better about my blunder, so you can feel better too if you've made the same ones:

Mistyping is Common

Almost everyone will mistype, and that is okay. It is a part of the self-discovery process as you explore who you are. Still, it is essential to know how prevalent it is because then you can expect it and not be so quick to get your Enneagram number tattooed on your ankle and flaunt it around.

You can also count on other people possibly being mistyped themselves. Hold yourself back when you start trying to walk a mile in their shoes by borrowing their *Personality Paintbrush*. It might be a distorted perspective.

Typing is Theory

Typing yourself by yourself is still technically theory since the details of your unconscious mind aren't accessible to your conscious mind without introducing another party into the mix to give you clues. Take a doctor who studies the spleen, for example. If you lived in a bubble without access to other humans, including their knowledge, you would live and die, never knowing you even had a spleen, yet there it would be working in the background orchestrated by your brain, keeping you alive.

The doctor can explain to you what your spleen does. Still, that's only spleen theory and may or may not apply to your actual spleen. The real functioning of your spleen might deviate from its expected functioning, depending on the health of your spleen and the stress placed on it. This same idea applies to your Core Type, which leads us to the third fact about mistyping.

Tests are Not Accurate

Tests are only 50-60% accurate. That's basically a coin toss! The inaccuracy is not the test's fault. But the very nature of human psychology and how we create our current reality sets us up to be overconfident in answering questions on an Enneagram test.

Typing yourself is even trickier because your brain sometimes has difficulty distinguishing between perception and reality. Sometimes, you answer the questions based on how you perceive yourself (or how you are when you like yourself) versus how you actually are, warts and all. Ever watch the American Idol auditions and ask yourself, "You call that singing? Can he not hear himself?" Or, when you say, "I used to be late all of the time, but I've gotten better." That may be true, but you're still late most of the time.

Your conclusions are determined by how you interpret situations, and your past experiences or conditioning play a considerable role in that interpretation. If your thinking is bogged down by distorted images, illogical reasoning, or jumping to wrong conclusions, you become blind to the truth or reality of the situation. This isn't usually intentional. It's one of the ways your brain protects you, but it is also one of the ways your brain can hinder you when you are unaware of your own *Experience Gap* within yourself.

Transparent moment: I used to have a free questionnaire on my website. Being a statistician, I tried extremely hard to include questions that spoke to the triads and motivations of each type, but people were still confused by their results, so I took it down! Self-reported data is not reliable.

Also, most people who only take an online test as their sole means of discovering their type will only study the type the test assigned to them, like Dennis. Typing correctly by the process of elimination involves understanding ALL nine types to rank the core motivations as they pertain to you.

"Mistyping occurs from a lack of
understanding of the top-down infrastructure
of the Enneagram."

"So, typing is a process of elimination. Got it. What else?"

Mistyping occurs from a lack of understanding of the top-down infrastructure of the Enneagram. It also happens if you are unaware of how your brain's conscious perceptions are not accurate, especially if not given boundaries or context.

So, in addition to the process of elimination, you also have to follow the rules of the game. If you were an online-test taker, you probably didn't know there were rules, or you trusted the quiz already took those rules into account.

There are only three rules, but each one points to an essential part of the infrastructure of the Enneagram system. Let's go over the rules more closely to examine how they support the framework of the system and how your brain tricks you when you are taking an assessment.

Rule #1: Your Core Type is determined by your MOTIVATIONS, not your behaviors.

This is the #1 Rule of Enneagram Typing, and it is the #1 Rule that is most broken. So go ahead and put this rule on repeat on your playlist. This isn't willful rule-breaking though, but just how human psychology works.

The entire infrastructure of the Enneagram rests on WHY you behave the way you do. Not the actual behaviors themselves. Your psyche is wired to search for meaningful patterns in everything. However, two people can express the same behavior for two completely different reasons.

Remember that the language of the subconscious uses emotions and symbols. You think in pictures, and once you "see" something in your mind's eye, it can be hard to "unsee" it. For example, if I say to you, DO NOT think of a pink elephant, your mind immediately thinks of a pink elephant, even if it was for just a split second! Because you have to imagine what a pink elephant looks like to NOT think of it.

Likewise, when you read a question on a test or a description in a book, you're likely imagining or remembering a time when you or someone else was doing the thing. For example, if you are asked, "Do you want to be neat and tidy?" your mind starts picturing all the things you do that prove you are neat and tidy (or not neat and tidy, if that may be the case). You have a different idea or level of tolerance of what neat and tidy means to you.

But guess what? That's behavior! Behaviors are actions you can see or imagine. Motivations are intentions associated with intense feelings of desires and fears. You can't see or imagine an intention or emotion. What you really should be asking yourself is, "Why is being neat and tidy important to you?" or "How strong is your desire to be neat and tidy?" (aaaaand answer yourself honestly. Ouch!)

A **Type 2** might say, because it makes people feel welcomed.

A **Type 3** might say, because it makes me look good.

A **Type 4** might say, because it is aesthetically pleasing.

A **Type 5** might say, it isn't important as long as I know where my favorite stuff is.

A **Type 6** might say, because I know where things are just in case I need them.

A **Type 7** might say, because I get distracted otherwise.

A **Type 8** might say, because I like to be in control of my environment.

A **Type 9** might say, because it's important to my wife.

A **Type 1** might say, because I should be neat and tidy.

This isn't representative of every person of that type; remember, personality is a spectrum, a continuum of behaviors. But your core motivations won't vary much.

Now, other personality system assessments are not necessarily more superior systems just because they might be more accurate at typing you on their system. Those assessments measure behaviors to help you discover a personality profile that is determined by behaviors, which are easier to recognize. But it's your motivations that determine your Enneagram Type, and your core motivations are deeply rooted in the fabric of your psyche. Some of them you are aware of, and some are unconscious and take some exploring with a coach, therapist, partner, or friend.

See how online tests can get tricky?

You click the answers according to the images you conjure up in your mind, and in your rush to get through an online test, sadly, you get mistyped. Determining one's motivations takes some digging and can't reliably happen in the twenty minutes it takes to answer a few questions from a Bot.

We can behave like another Enneagram number for three major reasons:

Wings

First, each number has two Wing Subtypes on either side of your Core Type, where you can access the stereotypical behaviors of either, neither, or both *wings*. See the chart below. As a Type 7, I'm optimistic and adventurous, but when I was a parent of littles, I would "dip" into the Type 6 behaviors of hypervigilance when taking the kids somewhere new that might trigger a meltdown. Likewise, I would bring out the Type 8 behaviors of toughness and strength on the co-ed soccer field, even though I've always been the smallest player by a lot. "I'm little, but I'm mean" was the motto I would mentally cast to opponents when they were surprised by my assertiveness. I'm sure from the stands, it was comical to watch 5-foot me challenge 6-foot fellows.

Stress and Security Numbers

Second, each number has a Stress Path and a Security Path, where you take on the stereotypical behaviors of a different number depending on your stress level. Between your *Core Type*, *Stress Number*, *Security Number*, and two *Wings*, that's a total of five types that we can easily and intuitively behave like at any given moment of the day.

As you can see from the chart, if you are a Type 8 under stress, you will take on the stereotypical behaviors of your Stress Number, Type 5, and isolate yourself to make observations of your environment, but as a means of maintaining your strength of will. Under extreme stress, this might be going "underground" as an overcompensating drive to protect yourself from enemies or regain control of your environment. Unhealthy responses under stress are called Disintegration.

Core Number	Wings		Stress Number	Security Number
8	7	9	5	2
9	8	1	6	3
1	9	2	4	7
2	1	3	8	4
3	2	4	9	6
4	3	5	2	1
5	4	6	7	8
6	5	7	3	9
7	6	8	1	5

However, Type 5 is the Security Number for the Type 7. So when I, as a Type 7, feel secure, I will be content with isolation with only the stimulation of thinking and researching. Assuming I'm not avoiding or escaping anything and am taking this time to grow myself, this is a healthy, secure response called Integration.

If we were hanging out in the basement, as a Type 7 and Type 8, together but apart in our own little worlds, we would show similar Type 5ish behaviors, but for different reasons. Not only would we have different motivations, but it might be a move toward Integration or growth for me and a move toward Disintegration for a Type 8. Your type's pattern of stress and security is unique to the type, so it is important not to be mistyped.

Instincts

And third, you have three *Instinctual Variant* subtypes for your number that follow the three survival instincts I mentioned in Chapter 2: self-preservation, sexual (social mate), and social (social order). Depending on the need you are trying to meet, your behaviors will shift, including doing the exact opposite of the stereotypical behaviors associated with your type. You'll learn about these *countertypes* in Chapter 11.

While I believe understanding the stress and security patterns of each type might be helpful to you on your typing journey, I generally warn my clients to stay away from Subtypes during Typing Mode. They are a dynamic part of your personality that can create more confusion and overwhelm, so I'll advise you to stick with the "top-down" approach and start at the Triad level of the hierarchy. More details on the best way to understand Triads in Chapter 7.

Regardless of your behaviors, they serve one purpose: To get what you want and avoid what you don't want. If you can imagine yourself doing it, it is a behavior. Ask yourself "Why?" until you discover the motivation behind the behavior.

Rule #2: You only have ONE Enneagram Type, and it never changes.

There is no double-dipping when it comes to your Core Type. You can't be a Type 1 and a Type 3. This rule is hard for many people to swallow because no one wants to be put into a box and told that you're stuck with this ONE personality... forever...

The truth is that we humans are great at creating coping skills. This might be mirroring skills where we model the behaviors we admire in others or the behaviors we convince ourselves will get us what we want in our current circumstances (or avoid what we don't want). These behaviors might be your style, habits, routines, or traditions you've adopted or adapted from your family or cultural traditions, or work conditions.

I was taught to make my bed every morning. And I loved walking in my parents' bedroom and seeing a made bed and a tidy room. It was calming, like when you first walked into a fancy hotel room. But I also like the freedom to not make my bed and not be hard on myself when I don't, like when I slept on the top bunk for two years in my college dorm. I never fixed my bed, and it was bliss. Now that I'm the one in the Master Bedroom, I try to make my bed every day, even if it isn't in the morning because I value a made bed and a tidy room. It isn't necessarily stereotypical Type 7 behavior, but it doesn't make me less of a Type 7. Your Enneagram Type is the anchor that grounds you and gives context to your ever-adapting behaviors.

Why is breaking this rule bad? Because the mentality of changing type profiles can nullify the Enneagram's intention for you to grow to be the best YOU, not to jump from one average type to the next average type. The Enneagram shows us a clear path already built into its infrastructure to move us forward on our personal growth journey toward Integration, and each type has its own unique Growth Path.

Now, if it's true that you are the same number now as you were when you were at age seven, stuffing M&Ms up your nose, how do we account for the differences in personality behaviors back then and how you behave now? (Assuming the M&Ms are only making it into your mouth now.)

Most psychologists believe that a child's personality regarding his self-esteem is developed during the first five years of life. At the beginning (and in general, if you're honest), you choose highly selfish coping strategies. But, snatching your brother's Thomas the Tank Engine without permission at age three is not considered willful stealing. You want it; you take it. And sometimes, get away with it.

Let's distinguish the difference between your type and your style. Your style is your preferred way of getting your core needs met and usually varies depending on which hat you're wearing. For example, learning style is your style when you are the student, and your teaching style is when you are the teacher, and these can be different sets of behaviors. These, along with your parenting, friendship and leadership styles, and so on, are usually modeled to us. Your attachment style is developed in response to your experiences with relationships, beginning with your mother figure or caretaker. Style is not set in stone but is your preferred strategy of getting your needs met in the roles you play. Left to its own devices, this part of your personality will "follow the dopamine" as you navigate the rewards and punishments (real or perceived) in your life.

As you mature, you learn that your actions affect the world around you and not always in a good way. And perhaps even come back to bite you in the rear (Sometimes literally in our house, especially if it involves snatching Thomas.). So you learn to adapt to become better, and over time, you develop your character. Your character is the part of your personality style that involves your morals and the personal growth and integrity you've learned through your experiences.

The *Ladder of Awareness* is the symbol for your personal growth and development. The higher you climb, the more awareness you gain, the more access to healthy or mature responses you can make.

At the bottom rungs are your unhealthy behaviors, and at the top rungs of the ladder are your healthy behaviors. When you aren't thinking about your personality, you hang out on the middle rungs, in your "average" behaviors. These are the stereotypical behaviors you default to — they are neither healthy nor unhealthy.

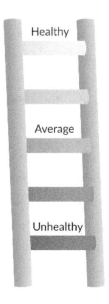

Each of the nine Types has its own ladder template with nine rungs, three rungs for each category of healthy, average, and unhealthy. These are your *Levels of Health*, also called Levels of Integration or Levels of Development (by Riso), and are unique to your Core Type. Yet another reason why it is so important to get your type right, first!

As you climb the ladder, you rise above the box of your personality ego and get a renewed perspective. Remember the symbol of Emmett standing proudly at the top of his LEGO® ladder? He has unboxed himself and has a great view and outlook on the world.

When you are at the bottom of the ladder, you only have a distorted perception of the world. Under stress, your extension ladder has been retracted, and the lid to your box has been shut. Imagine Emmett stuck in that LEGO® box with only a tiny window on one wall to view the world through.

Restricted by this narrow view with only your average and unhealthy behaviors readily accessible, you feel stuck. But the ladder is still available in your box within your reach. You just need to decide to pick it up, open the lid, and climb out.

Your character explains why you no longer do childish things. But going back to Rule #1, remember that your core motivations solely determine your Enneagram number. That seed is consistent throughout your lifespan. So, when you're thinking about what Enneagram Type you might be, consider what motivated you as a child, a young adult when you first became independent, and at your current age. Your behaviors will have changed over time, but you will see a common thread of the why behind them if you take the time to reflect.

Rule #3: Use the NUMBERS, not the labels, to avoid wrongfully stereotyping.

As the Enneagram became more popular, influencers have given each type a label to help better explain the types' average behaviors. But remember, I said that these are the behaviors you show when you aren't thinking about your personality. So logically, why would you consider using these labels to help you correctly identify your Enneagram Type?

Winnie came to her typing session with me already convinced she was a Type 2. When I asked how she came to that conclusion, she said, "I'm a caretaker. I take care of people. People have always told me how helpful I am. Ever since I was a little girl, I've loved helping people and taking care of them. That's why I became a nurse." Spoiler Alert, Winnie is not a Type 2. She thought she was a Type 2 because the chapter in one of her books for Type 2 was titled "The Helper," and a blog article she read called the Type 2 "The Caretaker," which was the exact vocabulary she and others have used to describe her for her entire life.

Now the intentions of the labeling were innocent and served the early scholars well with an association for quick retrieval of an entire profile. In my humble opinion, the more people can understand the Enneagram faster and easier, the sooner we can establish world peace. But in the microwave mentality of today's world, to process things even faster, you can lose the nutrients that occur when you nuke something too long. You lose sight of the consequences of normalizing these labels.

When you use the labels, the nine types are no longer neutral. We all have our individual ideas of what it means to be an achiever, peacemaker, or epicure. And depending on our experiences, they can hold a positive or negative connotation that may cause us to gravitate towards (or repel) a particular label. You can mistype yourself like Winnie did if you focus too much on the label and not the motivations and stress patterns. Winnie did not become a nurse to nurture her patients; of course, she did take care of them, but her inner need is to support and advocate for their health. Winnie decided that she wanted to be more than a nurse who only takes care of people; she became a more prominent advocate for health and started an educational group for self-care.

Even if you are typed correctly, you can keep yourself in a box and stunt your personal growth by conforming to your perceptions of the label. And if using labels for describing your own type is boxing, it is even worse when you describe someone else's personality using a label. Your perceptions influence your expectations and can create a gap between how you experience each other in the average behavior space. And frequently, these labels muddy the waters when it comes to that *Experience Gap* and can create wedges in relationships.

"Jen, what is this Experience Gap you keep mentioning?"

Now that you've gotten a first exposure, or repetition, of some of the concepts and vocabulary I use in my coaching, you'll be happy to learn there is Glossary of Terms in the Appendix of this book. Use it as a quick reference for future spaced repetitions. It'll be handy as you come across these terms as you listen to the *Unbox Your Personality* podcast, or in the UBU Community on social media.

The term *Experience Gap* is typically used in business to describe when a brand doesn't meet the customer's expectations creating an overall unsatisfactory customer experience. In this book, I've used this analogy for relationships. It is when you make incorrect assumptions about the intention behind someone else's behaviors that can result in misunderstandings and unrealistic expectations, creating an overall unsatisfactory experience.

When I ask my son Eric a question, sometimes he doesn't acknowledge that I'm even in the room, much less actually answering me. He's a teenager now, so I think that's normal at this age, but even when he was younger, it was hard for me to get his attention.

"Do you want apples for a snack?" Crickets. And honestly, the first few times he did this, it did make me feel like he wasn't listening to me and was just ignoring me which is hard on a mama who had parenting insecurities.

I could be annoyed by his "disrespect" and say, "Hello?? McFly!" Or, I could be too forgiving and pull his autism card and make the snack for him anyway. Instead, I got in his line of sight between him and Thomas the Tank Engine and asked,

"Can you answer my question?"

"I did."

"Aloud?"

"Oh…"

I was experiencing neglect, rejection and disrespect of not feeling heard — but that was not his intention.

Sometimes the *Experience Gap* isn't so impactful that it causes issues in the relationship. You might not even be aware it is happening. This is because of your *Personality Paintbrush*. By default, you already start with an *Experience Gap* by "painting" your reality with your own cognitive biases, projecting your personality onto others in the form of predicting their behavior and assuming their intentions. All of the people-watching experiences I've done since I was a wee Jen have been merely my personality's interpretation of what was going on.

There are three different *Experience Gaps*:

- How you experience others vs.
  How they intend to be experienced

- How others experience you vs.
  How you intend to be experienced

- How you experience yourself being vs.
  How you intend to be (an *Experience Gap* within yourself)

Let's look at the brain science behind how this happens. You have mirror neurons that help you learn from other people through observation. The neurons translate someone else's behaviors into their intentions based on your current understanding of the world. Studies have shown that these neurons fire the same brain activity in your own brain when you watch someone wave as if you are also waving — even when you're not.

Your brain, wired for survival, automatically does this in order to protect you. It helps you predict their next move so you are ready to respond (even if your prediction isn't accurate). When someone leans in after a date, you might be expecting a kiss. How embarrassing when you go to pucker, and they lean in for a hug instead. Awkward. But if your date were a creep, you'd know to turn and run the other way. Survival!

You must also realize others have their own *Personality Paintbrush* and will make assumptions about your intentions as well that are based on their own cognitive biases. When their assumptions are wrong, it can make you feel boxed in. Closing that gap to connect deeper to build relationships feels vulnerable because it is exactly that. Transparency of your intentions can make you feel exposed, and your survival instincts rev up. When your partner isn't communicating their intentions directly, it can be frustrating and confusing trying to "read their mind," as your brain is constantly looking for the intentions of what's in your environment, including the meaning behind others' behaviors. Your partner is experiencing the same frustration when you aren't being transparent.

Even when you are being transparent with your intentions, you might have thick paint on your paintbrush, headstrong in your convictions about how you are experiencing yourself being. If you aren't careful, this can create an *Experience Gap* within yourself when your conscious intentions are not matched with your unconscious ones. This *Experience Gap* is created when your conscious focus is on your social and self needs, but your psyche is trying to get your survival needs met.

According to Maslow, your physiological and safety security needs must be met first, then your social and self needs (such as love, belonging, respect, self-esteem, and self-actualization). If there is a Gap within yourself, you are already dealing with not being safe — either physically, emotionally, or mentally — and your survival instincts have been alerted, with or without the presence of another person. This is the gap of being unbalanced and out of alignment with your core — a clue that you need to check under the hood to see if your *Personality Tripod* is stable.

If you are mistyped, trying to meet the core needs of the wrong type will only be temporarily satisfying, if it meets them at all. When I thought I was a Type 4, I was depressed and unable to reframe or find the silver linings for the grief I was experiencing over the miscarriage, my son's autism diagnosis, and my health issues. I'm grateful that believing I was a Type 4 permitted me to accept that suffering as part of my journey. I was able to stop and withdraw so I could feel those big feelings. But eventually

I fell further and further away from myself as I allowed myself to wallow too long.

Once I understood myself as a Type 7, it was like a veil was lifted. I was able to put my suffering into perspective and be grateful for what I had learned from my hard experiences instead of sad about them. I also had a context to behaviors that I could remember all the way back as a child that is more consistent with Type 7. Big personality, always on the go, always finding the fun, making people laugh, dare-devilish and adventurous, and honestly, a bit self-focused and childish. These are some things that I see missing in my life when I'm feeling that Gap within myself, and I can become more intentional about adding them back in so I feel more balanced.

If you're not chatting one-on-one with a coach, join a small group session in the UBU Community, or poll some friends and family to get insights into how they are experiencing you. Once you have been correctly typed on the Enneagram, you will be able to interpret your behaviors in the proper context of your core motivations and make the proper adjustments to meet your needs. Later in Chapter 13, you'll learn how to balance your *Personality Tripod* when your "check engine" light comes on, alerting you of a possible Gap within yourself.

PART III

7

UNDERSTANDING YOUR TRIAD TYPES AS COLORS

When I was six months pregnant with Eric, I got the nesting itch and believed I had to paint the whole house. Well, maybe not the entire house, but I suddenly had the energy to turn the house into a home for the family member I was growing.

The nursery, of course, had to be a happy place. With an outdoor theme in mind, the walls and ceiling turned into an expansive blue sky with puffy clouds floating across it. I laid down where the crib was to be assembled, and I imagined being him waking up in a grassy green-gingham-sheets field to the freedom and possibilities of an open sky above him. I couldn't wait to share my fascination with nature and God's creatures with my son. I added "bug" drawer pulls to the dresser, hung up "bee yourself" wall art, and I found the most adorable green rug with ants trekking across it from IKEA for future tummy time. It didn't occur to me at that moment that I could birth a homebody who hates bugs and grass.

We took regular pictures of Eric with his Boppy pillow for family to show how fast he was growing -- every week at first, then every month, then every year. The funniest "Boppy pictures" were the one where he started rolling over mid-picture, the one where he was sitting up and backward, and the one of just the Boppy pillow with his feet and diapered bum in the bottom corner as he was crawling out of the frame. Then one day, he rejected the Boppy completely, agitated just at the sight of it. The bees and dragonflies on its pillow cover no longer were happy to him.

It was a mystery until I discovered it was due to his hypersensitive hearing. He couldn't handle the buzzing of flying insects. A low threshold for auditory stimulation is a trait he inherited from me. I can only guess that his distaste of bugs and grass began to develop during an afternoon dose of vitamin D on a blanket in the yard during those early years. Maybe when a buzzing insect landed nearby, or worse, on him! I can't say for sure. Still, how can we both suffer from the same dysfunction and have different attitudes about the outdoors? I started nurturing him before he was even born to enjoy it. Even though we were cut from the same cloth, our personalities were still different. Ryan came along, and yet another personality variation was added to our home! He would have camped outside 24/7 if his allergies would have allowed it.

If the *Personality Spectrum* can vary so much within the same gene pool, imagine the possibilities outside of that.

Personality is like the color spectrum in so many ways than just the infinite number of colors. When you're watching a movie on your high-definition TV, the images are made up of millions of pixels, which are individual points or dots on your screen. Each pixel has three subpixels: red, green, and blue. By varying the intensity of each color within a dot, its RGB value, all of the other colors in the spectrum can be created from just these three colors. When you step away from the TV, all the dots merge and form the *Under the Sea* images on your screen when you watch

The Little Mermaid. Talk about the dynamic power of just three colors!

In the nursery, I wanted to add blades of grass to the bottom of the walls. When I went to the paint section at the home improvement store, I skipped right past the reds and the blues and went straight to the greens. Even so, there were a lot of greens to choose from. Each paint chip had three shades: light, medium, and dark. Once I picked my paint chip and shade, I then had to choose a finish: flat, matte, or glossy. Now I was ready to order my can of paint.

The more aware you are of the purpose of the paint, the less overwhelming it is to choose a color. I was painting grass, so I needed green. But I also knew the rest of the nursery had more muted tones, so I moved away from the kelly greens and toward the olive greens. It's a sunny room, so I chose matte. Done and done.

Like the paint chips, the Enneagram organizes all of the different personalities on the *Personality Spectrum*. You're given nine categories or types with similar characteristics instead of getting overwhelmed by the infinite combinations. Once you identify which category you belong to, you'll see so many differences even within the same category, some subtle and some stark!

Still, nine categories can be overwhelming. This is why I am such a strong proponent of understanding Triads. A triad is simply a set of three. When you are given three options, it is much easier to make a decision. Like in the story of Goldilocks, one will be "just right" compared to the other two.

The most popular triadic grouping of the Enneagram Types is the Centers of Intelligence, often referred to as simply the Centers, which describe your primary domain of experience of your world. The three groups are the Moving Center, the Feeling Center, and the Thinking Center. Like the pixels on your TV, you have all three, but one will have the most intensity.

These make up the RGB values of personality, and for that reason, I've assigned these colors to each group. Each color consists of three Enneagram Types that have common personality traits.

Red = Moving Center: the domain of your experiences is in your Physical Intelligence (Body). Red Types struggle with reality's impact on their autonomy and carry resistance, tension, and anger in their bodies. These are Types 8, 9, and 1.

Green = Feeling Center: the domain of your experiences is in your Emotional Intelligence (Heart). Green Types struggle with their self-image or identity and respond with exaggeration and shame about their authenticity and significance. These are Types 2, 3, and 4.

Blue = Thinking Center: the domain of your experiences is in your Mental Intelligence (Mind). Blue Types struggle with organizing their thoughts about their safety, security, or access to support, causing fear or anxiety about their stability. These are Types 5, 6, and 7.

When I jumped ship from Type 4 to Type 7, lightbulbs turned on because I backed up and directed my focus to the Triad level, looking at the traits that are associated with each Center. I didn't shed a single tear, but I felt the anticipatory anxiety just thinking about the nuclear attack on Hiroshima. Since that was an automatic anxiety response versus an emotional response, I was more likely to be a Blue Type (5, 6, or 7) instead of a Green Type. And my Enneagram teacher and mentor coached me to help me figure out that I'm actually a Type 7.

Ironically, this was a type I had dismissed when I tried to type myself by myself. I never saw myself as a Type 7 because of the caricature depictions of the Type 7 on social media. Months later, I still would catch myself questioning it, unable to shake or unlearn what I thought it meant to be a Type 7. But focusing on the process of elimination, Type 7 fits the best, even if I don't agree with everything I read about Type 7 behaviors. It turns out, many of the discrepancies were due to the blind spots I had to overcome.

After a few months of using the "Start with your Centers" approach in my business, I was surprised at how many people had also mistyped themselves for the same reason. I had clients that went from a Type 9 to a Type 2, or a Type 6 to a Type 8, or a Type 3 to a Type 7 simply by learning about the traits of the Centers.

But it wasn't enough. A few people still struggled with which Center is their Dominant Center. After all, we all have a body, heart, and mind.

"But I see myself in all three, Jen!"

And truthfully, that isn't necessarily a bad thing. *Personality Wellness* isn't just about the deep explorations of your parts, but also being a more whole integrated you. But sometimes, when it comes to finding your Enneagram Type, it can be frustrating to parse it out. Some types are aware, but some are unaware, or they might be aware but unaccepting (like I was). The "aware" types don't seem to struggle as much to identify their Centers of Intelligence. But the "unaware" and "unaccepting" types seem to waver or have false confidence about which Center of Intelligence is their main one.

For example, according to the methodology, Natasha self-identified as a feeler, a Green Type, which means she was likely a 2, 3, or 4. But she didn't quite feel like she fit any of the types. Since Type 2 was the closest, she decided to "try on the Type 2 cape" for a week to see how it fit. A few days later, I was getting messages about how she didn't agree with most of the profile for the Type 2 but she knew, without a doubt, she's a "feeler."

I thought to myself, "There's got to be a more systematic way to do this." In my attempt to find a more reliable method, I went to the other extreme and made it way too complicated, adding more Triads, Subtypes, and theories that most people hadn't even heard of. It only took a couple of three-hour sessions and a few clients abandoning their follow-ups for me to realize that I had overdone it. Their brains were fried, or they just didn't have the time to get a master's degree in psychology to be able to follow my logic.

"With the 9AL™, I've made understanding your personality's nature simpler without losing the power of the Enneagram."

And that's how the 9 Acknowledgment Languages (9AL)™ were born! I took the two most popular Triad Groups of the Enneagram, The Centers and Stances, and that's it! I cut out the Wings, the Instincts, the Object Relations childhood theories and *overlays* that made my clients' eyes puddle and just stuck to nine characteristics about themselves on which they could focus. With the 9AL™, I've made understanding your personality's nature simpler without losing the power of the Enneagram.

The *Stances* of the Enneagram are loosely based on the work of psychoanalyst Karen Horney (pronounced horn-eye), who developed the most popular theory of the reactions to needs in relationships. Stances describe your posture, attitude, or standpoint for getting your needs met. They are the Withdrawn Stance, Aggressive Stance, and Dependent Stance.

Based on the CMY color model of pigments, I assigned the Stances the colors cyan, magenta, and yellow, to show that a combination of these three colors can also derive every personality on the spectrum.

Your inkjet color printer uses the CMY color model. You'll see three separate docks when you open up the cover to replace the ink cartridges. One port for cyan, one for magenta, and one for yellow (some have a 4th for black ink, which saves you a lot of moolah on colored ink, not having to use them to create the color black). Your printer mixes these three inks and produces all of the colors you need to make copies of your favorite vacation pictures that you want to put in your scrapbooks.

Again, each stance color consists of three Enneagram Types that have common personality traits.

Cyan = Withdrawn Stance: you move away from people to get your needs met. These are Types 9, 4, and 5.

Magenta = Aggressive Stance: you move against people to get your needs met. These are Types 8, 3, and 7.

Yellow = Dependent Stance: you move towards people to get your needs met. These are Types 1, 2, and 6.

There are other common traits within a stance, including blind spots. I'll cover this in Chapter 10.

At first, I assigned the colors strictly as a metaphor to help people distinguish between the triad groups. Still, there are so many powerful connections between how colors behave and how humans behave that I've discovered through the theory of colors that have helped my students make quick associations to memorize which type is which. But that's for another book!

Natasha gave me a second chance and showed up for her follow-up. We backed up and started over just using the Centers and Stances, and she successfully identified with Type 6, which happens to be a type that is not as aware of their Center of Intelligence. That's why just looking at the Centers didn't work for her.

I needed a framework that incorporated both the Centers and Stances triad traits, which evolved as the 9 Acknowledgment Languages (9AL)™. This concept was developed for an online course at Unbox University (UBU), originally called "How to Communicate to Build Relationships." It started as a guide for business owners to build rapport with their customers and clients when they don't know the Enneagram Type of the other party. It is now a small group course and online workshop for leaders (business, teachers, coaches, parents, mentors, etc.) who want to reconnect with their own Acknowledgment Languages so they can connect and lead more authentically and be the role model they aspire to be, professionally and personally.

> *"On a personal level, this program has helped me to better understand my husband and children, which has strengthened my relationships with them. And learning more about how and why I'm wired has helped me give myself grace as I strengthen my superpowers, without being distracted by the numbers!"*
> *says UBU student Lea Jacobson, CCA, and founder of the Essential Oil Safety Academy.*

The 9AL™ became the foundational theory taught in the UBU Coach Certification program for aspiring coaches who want to effectively use the Enneagram with their clients. So, if you are not 100% sure which Enneagram Type you are yet, the following chapters will help bring you more confidence for eliminating the types you definitely cannot be.

Instead of only looking at the 9AL™ in the context of your relationships, you'll see an alternative approach, using the context of your survival and comfort, or self-protection reflexes. Just like your knee-jerk reflex must go to completion once activated by a stimulus, so does your *Personality Reflex*. And the 9AL™ give you a clear illustration of how that process works.

8

Understanding Your Personality Reflexes (9AL™)

Our Christmas tree is one of my favorite things to decorate for the holidays. Each ornament is like a page in a scrapbook that I get to flip through once a year and remember the life we've built together as a family.

Back in 1996, there was only one ornament on our scrawny little tree standing in front of the sliding glass door of our first apartment. It was from Hallmark and read "Our First Christmas" with a picture of Terry and me with our impossibly young newlywed faces.

Since then, every milestone, every vacation, and every meaningful ornament purchased or gifted to us would get a place on the tree. As you can imagine, our 10-foot tree is getting crowded after twenty-five years, two kids, and plenty o' pets later! I'll catch myself or one of the boys stop at the tree and just reminisce about our adventures all season long.

Sometimes, like for our mission trip to Jordan, we weren't able to find a Christmas ornament, so I bought a tiny stuffed camel, used my Cricut to iron on the date, and sewed a hook onto it.

When I pick up that camel, I immediately smile, as I'm transported back onto the camel I rode through the desert and many other memories of my experience there. I remember our hosts wouldn't let us sleep when we got off the plane in order to "power through" the jet lag. I remember riding a donkey up the mountain at Petra and desperately feeling like I needed a seatbelt so I wouldn't fall off the cliff. I remember the hospitality and joy on the faces of the refugee families we visited even while they were sharing their heartbreaking stories with us. And a multitude of other emotions and stories would come to mind — until ten seconds later when I hear, "Mom! Mom! Mom! Remember this one? When we went to the tractor place? That was so fun!" With my reverie broken, I switched my sets of memories to the John-Deere field trip.

Isn't it amazing how one stimulus can trigger a series of responses for you? Remembering is validating. In a fraction of a second, all of those memories and emotions seem to all come flooding into your conscious aware ness, saying this actually happened and this is how you felt about it. "Yes, it was really fun. Remember how small you were standing in that huge tractor wheel?"

However, there is a much bigger picture to see here. It's the unconscious functions that you often forget to validate. Have you ever caught yourself holding your breath in anticipation, or breathing harder as you hike up a mountain? You typically don't notice until you're out of breath or your friend suggests you both slow down and pace yourselves. When was the last time you appreciated your lungs? Or, your intestines or liver, for that matter? When you duck to miss bumping your head, do you ever thank your brain for recognizing you were approaching a low-hanging branch? In approximately 1.2 seconds, you will need to hunch your back and bend your knees at least twenty degrees to clear that branch, without even the slightest break in the engaging conversation you're having with your hiking friend. Chances are you probably didn't even notice any of that. It was just a reflex.

Of the eleven million bits of information that your brain takes in per second, only about fifty of them are registered by your conscious mind. That's just .0004% of all the information you actually sensed from your environment! This means 99.9996% of your brain's processing is happening "under the radar," helping you prevent concussions from branches and other survival priorities, like pumping blood, digesting your s'mores, healing bug bites, and growing claws – I mean, toenails – without needing to interrupt your train of thought or your focus. While your conscious motivation or focus might be exercising, exploring, or simply conversing with your friend, your body is governed by your unconscious mind. It is always and solely busy focusing on keeping you alive or returning you to homeostasis.

When my son Ryan burned himself on the stove, he didn't have to consciously decide to jump back to remove the source of pain. That reflex happened before he was even aware of what had happened. Your personality is triggered in the same way. You have unconscious responses to your environment that occur before you are aware of it. Some of your responses are conditioned, but the Enneagram helps you identify the hardwired responses in your brain.

That hardwiring is your personality's primal self-protection reflexes. In this chapter, we are going to examine the primitive components of these reflexes: how your Enneagram Type processes information from your environment (like a tree branch), and the external response (like ducking), and more importantly, the blind spots that your Enneagram Type has that trick you into thinking there's a branch to duck under when there actually isn't.

It might be hard to wrap your brain around the exact science of how your body grows toenails, but it is something that we accept because of the hard evidence of your growing nails. Unsightly as they may be if left au natural, they do serve a purpose! They are designed to protect your sensitive toes by curving down over the front where they often get stubbed. However, with the invention of socks and shoes to do that protection for you, you are left with the task of clipping them to prevent them from becoming ingrown and painful. And you likely never made the connection that this pain results from denying your body's natural process to protect your piggies.

The nature of your personality is the same way. The exact science has been hard to report. The combination of genes that make up your personality on the inside is just as diverse as the combination of genes that make up your appearance on the outside. There have been countless twin studies showing that genetics are more influential in shaping temperament when comparing identical to fraternal sets. In one study at the University of Edinburgh, Professor Timothy Bates concluded that the genetic influence was strongest on a person's sense of self-control (Dopamine, anyone?).

But unlike toenail growth, the evidence of your personality's primal self-protection is not so obvious –– Professor Bates needed 800 sets of twins to come to his conclusion. Your personality might be unsightly if left au natural, but it does serve a purpose! Acknowledging its role in your survival instincts brings about a more profound respect to yourself and your hardwired abilities that you often take for granted.

In 2015, I badly broke my left leg during a soccer game. Talk about taking the role of something for granted! The tibia bone at the knee joint had been smashed and required a metal plate and 6 screws to reattach. I was non-weight bearing restricted for 6 weeks and had many long months of recovery afterward with a fully braced leg and crutches or cane. In order to be mobile, my body started adapting to a new center of gravity, compensating for not being able to use or bend my left leg.

However, when I regained enough function of my leg to walk on my own, my body protested. It had slowly shifted to its new normal of homeostasis during those months, and now I needed to shift back to my regular normal. Unfortunately, my posture was so far out of alignment from leaning on crutches or a cane that it was more comfortable to be crooked; my right leg was much stronger, and I continued to allow it to do all of the work. Because I was "off" and unbalanced, it was hard for me to do the things I could do before. At one point, my goal was just to be able to sit criss-cross applesauce on the floor because my knee "forgot" how to bend. We could talk about soccer once I learned how to relax without needing to be completely horizontal.

While the first shift of my body's adaptation was due to the necessity for survival and comfort, this second shift was not. It would take a lot of conscious effort and pain to return to my original design, and it is still an ongoing journey. But I know, by being intentional and consistent, that eventually it will take less effort, and I will have less pain, and I can get back to living life the way I'm meant to live.

It sounds a lot like your personal growth journey and getting back to your core self, doesn't it? But I didn't try to recover on my own. I wouldn't have known where to start. Physical therapy and chiropractic sessions were needed to show me how my body is supposed to function and what exercises I needed to do to get back to my natural way of moving.

This is why the 9 Acknowledgment Languages (9AL)™ for your Enneagram Type is so practical. It goes back to your core or root or origin and acknowledges your most natural way of being and interacting in the world. Below is the list of your nine languages, but this isn't a pick and choose list that matches one-to-one with an Enneagram number. Your type's *Personality Reflex* is to speak all nine languages in your own specific dialect, which I will describe in the following chapters.

> *"The 9AL™ takes the common traits of the two most popular Triads of the Enneagram: Centers of Intelligence and Hornevian Stances, or simply the Centers and the Stances."*

9 Acknowledgment Languages (9AL)™

1. Experience Gate

2. Attention Filter

3. Emotional Yardstick

4. Control Tactic

5. Social Style

6. Pace Style

7. Timeline Focus

8. Timeline Blind Spot

9. Center Blind Spot

By looking at these primitive components of the psychology of your *Personality Reflex*, you'll be able to validate the process your psyche is playing out naturally. Understanding your personality at its core will give you a new perspective to identify what pieces of your basic wiring you've been working against that are sabotaging your efforts — allowing you to be more intentional and heal so you feel more balanced and whole.

Additionally, you'll be aware of the red flags that something isn't fully functioning. While I was in Jordan, post-broken-leg era, we were stuck on the side of the road with van troubles. As we waited for help, someone brought out a soccer ball, and we went into the desert to pass the time. It had been a year since I had played soccer on that fateful day, so I was excited to get back in the game, so to speak. My brain would tell my body to trap the ball coming toward me, but my body's reflexes were a bit too slow. I was spending more time chasing balls I had missed than actually playing. I could have been down on myself about being "broken" and being a "failure" and "never being able" to play soccer again (and if I'm honest, there was a lot of that going on on the inside). But this was actually the red flag that warned me I was "off" and set me on the path of real recovery. And that is what the 9AL™ can do for you.

The point of focusing on the 9AL™ serves two purposes:

1. ***To redirect the focus away from the stereotypical outward behaviors of your Enneagram Type.***

Too many people believe that those are fixed traits (Newsflash! They're not, just the default ones), which leads to judgment and misdirected efforts that are fruitless.

Speaking of fruits, I was at the grocery store one day and apples were on the list. Before each choice, I picked up one apple and examined it for knicks, bruises, and firmness. When I took it home and bit into it, it was not ripe and made my face get winky for a solid minute. I assumed all of the apples were ripe by default.

When you think about it, you can't see the apple's core from the outside. All you can see is the skin, its protective layer. If you took one each of a Granny Smith, Red Delicious, and Gala and removed their skins, it would be harder to tell which apple is which. You would have to "dig deeper" and experience the taste, smell, and texture of each for more clues.

If you take it one step further and eat or cut to the cores of each apple, you reach their seeds. Now they are even harder to distinguish. How can you judge one seed when they all look so similar at this level? All you really know is they are all apples.

The 9AL™ helps us to look at different personalities in this same way. When you dig to look at the seeds in your core, you're able to rise above the stereotypes of each Enneagram Type. This is climbing the *Ladder of Awareness*. At that higher view, you see a bigger picture, the larger goal, the commonalities among us, and how each of our roles fit together in the puzzle to complete the picture. You can have more empathy, compassion, and patience, having that common community goal. Because all you really know is that we are all human.

2. To identify the executive cognitive tools your brain uses to translate your experience into a language you understand.

You've heard of "lost in translation," right? When my cousin, Carina, moved to the United States after finishing college in the Philippines, she had to adjust to speaking English 90% of the time (not Taglish or Tagalog + English, which is only acceptable among other Filipinos). When I visited her a few years ago, we jumped on a call to chat with her brother still living in the Phils. He started speaking to me in Tagalog at full throttle. I sat there uncomfortably, only understanding every 15th word before raising my hand to request English. He laughed and apologized. Then came a long awkward silence as he had to pause and make a true effort to find the English words to communicate with me. My cousin empathized with her brother, saying, "It hurts your brain, right?" We got a good chuckle and continued the conversation, having Carina translate for us. But how limited we were! She could relay facts, like how big the kids are now, but why were they laughing so much? I'm sorry, but her translations just weren't that funny. I was probably missing out on some adorable story he told about what happened at breakfast that morning that would have really connected us on a parent level.

Each of the 9 Acknowledgment Languages™ has three dialects. You might be bilingual or trilingual, but one will be your primary dialect. Like your first or native language, it comes naturally to you. You fully comprehend and "speak" without needing to pause to translate since your brain does it automatically.

The 9AL™ are taken from the common traits of the Centers and the Stances. But instead of looking at them as personality traits to help you navigate relationships, I'm going to show you that they are actually the processing strategies used by the brain as communication tools, alerting you that your personality's primal self-protection reflexes have been triggered.

The first four languages of the 9AL™ are derived from the Centers and represent your internal processing reflex. I refer to them as your *Centers Reflex.*

The last five languages of the 9AL™ are derived from the Stances and represent three external responses and two blind spots. I refer to them as your *Stances Reflex.*

This is not an exclusive list of personality traits, of course. Other Triads represent additional internal, external, and blind spots for your type. Still, they are best examined and explored for you, as an individual, to have practical meaning in your own life's story.

For each language, we will specifically look at the survival role it plays in your brain and give examples of each dialect to make clear the distinctions. You'll also see how each Enneagram stereotype is affected by the fraction-of-a-second triggering of all nine of their Acknowledgment Languages when it comes to expressing their core motivations and fixations.

9

Understanding Your Internal Processing as a Reflex of Your Enneagram Type

Here begins the nerdy chapter you've been waiting for. It's totally worth having this base understanding of the inner workings of your Enneagram Type that most people miss or ignore. Don't worry if you haven't taken the 9 Acknowledgment Languages™ course yet. Think of this chapter and the next as the prequel to the course. You'll see each language on such a basic survival level that it will bring more clarity to the information you get from the course for building rapport in your relationships. Here in this book, you'll get a firmer grasp of what it means to just Be You.

Centers Reflex

The first four of the 9AL™ are the package of four traits that happen in an instant, broken down so you can understand how your unconscious mind causes you to behave. This is the first process when you come across new information (the stimulus) and follows a similar processing path as your conscious awareness: Sensory → Attention → Rehearsal → Retrieval, but on an unconscious level as a primal self-protection reflex.

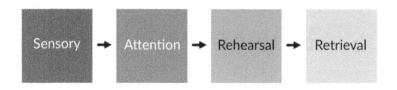

They form your *Centers Reflex* and are called:

1. Experience Gate - how input is experienced or sensed

2. Attention Filter - what grabs your attention

3. Emotional Yardstick - how you remember an experience

4. Control Tactic - how you decide to manage it

The *Centers Reflex* is all internal, before you've had a chance to respond or react, and more importantly, before you've had an opportunity to adapt or conform to your nurtured personality. If you had nine people in a classroom, each of a different Enneagram Type, and a wasp suddenly appeared and began buzzing around, there would be nine different processes going on in their minds. However, their ultimate behavior of responding to the wasp might not necessarily be nine different responses. It will depend on their stress level, awareness level, and the nurtured part of their personality. For example, all those with an allergy to wasps might be withdrawing and checking if their epi-pens are nearby, regardless of their Enneagram Type.

You'll also see this difference in behaviors within types. A Type 8 with an allergy to wasps would react completely differently from a Type 8 who does not have an allergy. Therefore, you can't assume you know what is going on in someone's head based on their behavior. The extreme illustration of this is to imagine all nine people were completely paralyzed and unable to move or communicate. The stimulus of the wasp would trigger their nine different thought processes, but all nine of them would have the exact same response: sitting still, saying nothing. Yet, we know that they still have a personality with feelings, thoughts, desires, and fears. This affirms the value of the Enneagram, knowing that your type is determined by your internal core motivations versus your outer behaviors.

Let's review the Centers of Intelligence triad groups:

Moving Center = the domain of your experiences is in your Physical Intelligence (Body). Red Types struggle with the impact that reality has on their autonomy and carry resistance, tension, and anger in their bodies. These are the "Red" Types 8, 9, and 1.

Feeling Center = the domain of your experiences is in your Emotional Intelligence (Heart). Green Types struggle with their self-image or identity and respond with exaggeration and shame about their authenticity and significance. These are the "Green" Types 2, 3, and 4.

Thinking Center = the domain of your experiences is in your Mental Intelligence (Mind). Blue Types struggle with organizing their thoughts about their safety, security, or access to support, causing fear or anxiety about their stability. These are the "Blue" Types 5, 6, and 7.

When triggered, all four languages speak within a fraction of a second of each other. However, we will look at each of them individually so you can understand the role each one serves in your internal processing. For illustrative purposes, I will describe external reactions in the examples in this chapter. You'll know they are external reactions because I'll change the tense to the future tense.

Experience Gate

Think of your house. You have a front door, a back door, and a side door. You can come and go through any door, but one door gets used the most. For example, I almost always use the side door from the garage in my home, but because my neighbors park on the street, they always enter their home through their front door.

The thalamus in your brain receives the sensory input of your environment. Your *Experience Gate* translates the input into the language of how you experience the information through your body, heart, or mind.

If you are Body-Dominant, meaning it is your primary or native dialect, you experience incoming information through physical sensations or energy, physiological needs, and your actions or movements. When the wasp enters the room, you'll likely first sense its proximity to your body, listening to the buzz of its wings or trying to keep your eyes on the target. You'll feel compelled to help the situation by taking action or noticing what the others in the room are doing.

If you are Heart-Dominant, you are more attuned to emotional needs. Instead, you would first experience the wasp incident by the emotions in the room. Maybe you'll tell yourself, "I'm ok," or reassure others or crack a joke if people are freaking out. You might also take action like the Body Types, but you'll return to your primary dialect of meeting emotional needs (your own or others') by noticing if there's still an emotional charge in the room.

If you are Mind-Dominant, your focus will be on your thoughts, beliefs, and ideas. In this scenario, you likely would stay in your head first. You'll feel compelled to ask questions, "What is that, a wasp?" "How did the wasp even get in here?" "Is anyone here allergic to wasps?" or make statements about your beliefs like "Wasps are harmless if you don't anger them." Again, you'll still take action or ask if people are ok and calm them, but you will keep feeling compelled to find out the what, how, and why to make logical sense of the situation.

Same situation, three different experiences. You can use all three gates, but your primary dialect is the one that takes less effort or the one you keep returning to. In other words, it is the most comfortable, therefore the most convenient. I enter my home through the side door coming in from the garage in my house because it is the one that makes the most sense to me. It is also the path of least resistance. Of course, I could walk out my front door. But then I would have to walk all the way around to the side of the house, up the driveway, and open the garage door to get to my car. Doable, but not preferable.

Attention Filter

If your *Experience Gate* is how you receive information from the world, the *Attention Filter* is how you filter that information.

Remember my LEGO® box? When Emmett, the mini-figure, is inside the box at the bottom of his *Ladder of Awareness*, he could only see out of the small tinted window. When you are stuck in your boxes, you are limited to this one view out of this one window on this one wall. You are blind to everything else. It is an incomplete view and often a distorted reality and prevents you from seeing the bigger picture.

The parable of the blind men and the elephant illustrates this distorted reality:

> *A group of blind men heard that a strange animal, called an elephant, had been brought to the town, but none of them were aware of its shape and form. Out of curiosity, they said, "We must inspect and know it by touch." So, they sought it out, and when they found it, they groped about it. The first person, whose hand landed on the trunk, said, "This being is like a thick snake." It*

seemed like a kind of fan for another one whose hand reached its ear. As for another person, whose hand was upon its leg, he said, "The elephant is a pillar-like a tree trunk." The blind man who placed his hand upon its side said, "The elephant is a wall." Another who felt its tail described it as a rope. The last man felt its tusk, described the elephant as hard, smooth, and like a spear.

Your *Attention Filter* is the tinting on that window that colors your perspective in a specific way, similar to the idea of rose-colored glasses. It tells your brain, "Hey, I notice there's 'rosy' information here." And what you don't notice... you don't notice. You forget or become unaware of any "non-rosiness" in your environment. Just like the blind men with the elephant, you "grope" the world that is right in front of you. But instead of being blind, you are just looking out of your one small window that translates the incoming information and filters it according to what gets your attention and what doesn't.

The amygdala in your brain is responsible for detecting threatening stimuli. Depending on your dialect, you use your *Attention Filter* to scan your environment for any threats to your impact, image, or security.

If you are Impact-Dominant, you are scanning your environment for any threatening impact on your autonomy. You pay attention to the information you need or want to be involved in, as well as how other people's involvement impacts your autonomy. If the wasp seemed to only linger in the opposite corner of the room, or someone opened a window to shoo it out, it is something you can "forget," meaning you don't need to get involved because you are not physically impacted. But if the wasp was lingering above you buzzing too loudly, or worse, landed on you, you have been impacted, and this situation now has your attention.

If you are Image-Dominant, you are scanning for threats to your reputation or significance, especially if you feel your image might not be seen as authentic. If the person next to you screams and looks to you to be the hero, you'll go after the wasp to try to save the day. Or, if you want to be seen as the "cool one in a crisis," you'll downplay how heartbroken you are over everyone attacking the poor wasp who was probably just afraid. You pay attention to opportunities to maintain the image of how you want to be seen.

If you are Security-Dominant, you are scanning for threats to the safety of your mental stability, including how other people's insecurities might affect your own security. If everyone was calm and collected while taking care of the wasp situation, or the crisis was quickly averted and there was no harm done, this experience would probably become "forgettable" or lumped together with the other "encounters with wasps" memories. But people are swatting and screaming, despite you telling them to "just stand still and you won't get stung." Your attention is won because you know the wasp is angry now and more likely to attack back in defense.

You probably are starting to notice how these first four Acknowledgment Languages work together in lightning succession. For example, if you are Impact-Dominant, you automatically notice the impact on your (and that of others) ability to be autonomous, to move your body, or perform actions without help. Likewise, if you're Image-Dominant, you pay attention to emotional needs to feel significant, to be seen. And if you're Security-Dominant, you are projecting your beliefs and ideas, so you feel stable or confident.

Neat, huh? But wait! There's more...

Emotional Yardstick

It has the word "emotional" in its name — that might sound vulnerable, powerless, gooey, or out of control. But that isn't the role emotions play in your unconscious mind.

Remember reading that there are two main rehearsal strategies to improve memory: repetition and association. The hippocampus in your brain takes new input and either connects it to prior repetitions or associates it to similar experiences. New input with no previous exposure must create a new association. In order to be stored in long-term memory, the strongest native association tool you have are your emotions. The hippocampus uses the signals from the amygdala to encode emotion into your long-term memories, which is why you remember the events of your past that have an emotional impact on you.

So how does this work? Once you receive new information through your *Experience Gate* and your *Attention Filter* notices it, your *Emotional Yardstick* tells your brain which experiences you will remember by assigning an emotional value using the continuums of anger, shame, or fear.

At its most primitive and detached function, this language is not about how you emotionally respond to incoming information with anger, shame, or fear, but how you measure and judge which experiences get stored in your memory. It's as emotionally neutral as how you measure distance in yards (or meters) or loudness in decibels.

When you assign a high value or intensity to an experience, it becomes memorable and likely because it is associated with one of the legs of your *Personality Tripod* (Core Motivations, Core Strengths, Core Values). If you don't care about the new information, you'll assign it a low value ("meh") or no value at all, and you won't respond or remember it. The higher this assigned value, the faster the recall or retrieval you'll have in the next processing step after the *Emotional Yardstick*.

If you are Anger-Dominant, the level of emotion you assign to your experience of being impacted falls somewhere between "bothered" or "bitter" to "rage" or "passion." If you are more irritated about the wasp being in your space, you'll remember more details about the whereabouts of the insect than the chaos of the people. But suppose you are passionate about the protection and conservation of wasps because of how they help farmers. In that case, you'll remember the details of the people's actions, like who was guilty or innocent in your eyes, or what they should've done instead. You might not feel the anger or passion as an emotion, but perhaps as heavy tension or energy in your body that wants to be released or is weighing you down. In some instances, you might label that sensation as shame or fear, but the primary emotion is on the anger continuum.

If you are Shame-Dominant, your *Emotional Yardstick* will range from a less intense value like bashfulness to varying intensity levels of pity, humiliation, guilt, or pride. If you are embarrassed by your attempt to swat at the wasp and missing it, you'll remember the details of what others saw or said about you. Or, if you were the one that "got 'im," you'll remember the details of the story of "the day I saved everyone from the killer wasp." This is not an incident you'll likely forget! On other occasions, you might be experiencing anger as "envy" or "self-loathing" and fear as "anxiety" or "worry" that you are not enough, but it will fall somewhere on the shame continuum.

"At its most primitive and detached function, this language is not about how you emotionally respond to incoming information with anger, shame, or fear, but how you measure and judge which experiences get stored in your memory."

If you are Fear-Dominant, you will measure your experiences in terms of the level of fear, from "wary" to "panic," or "anticipation" to "confidence." The more excitement you assign to the scene, the more details you'll remember about the sequence of events. You'll likely be able to call out the discrepancies between what's being told in the "day I saved everyone from the killer wasp" story and what actually happened. You might experience "confusion" or "timidity" or even "overconfidence" as shame/pride, and "defensiveness" "stressed out" or "passivity" as anger, but these emotions are also in the fear category.

The key to understanding the dialects of this language from a *Personality Reflex* perspective is to recognize that the purpose of this yardstick is not for emoting, but for processing what will become memories. Don't get distracted by speculating how each dialect might emotionally respond. This will be important for when you start implementing what you know about yourself and learning how to self-regulate in Chapter 13.

Control Tactic

Picture your brain as your computer's filing system, where each file is a memory or a bit of information you've learned in the past. As new information comes in, it needs to be managed. You probably have folders on your laptop to organize all the data in a way that makes sense to you. Maybe you have a folder per project. Perhaps you have a brilliant file naming system that is easily searchable (#goals). Or maybe your system is to download to your heart's content, back it up, wipe all your files and start fresh every year.

The prefrontal cortex of your brain is where your executive functions are carried out once your brain is done with its internal processing. Now that your *Centers Reflex* has entered the final phase of processing your experience, you are required to decide to carry out a function. Your dialect for the *Control Tactic* language is the primitive default tactic you use when you choose to manage or control the new information you've just experienced so that you can function and meet your needs.

Let's say you're looking for information on the internet. When you open your web browser (let's call that your *Experience Gate*) and search "how to treat a wasp sting" (that's like your *Attention Filter*), and a detailed infographic pops up in the search results. Perfect! Just what you were looking for. So you click to download it, saving it to your laptop's memory (like your *Emotional Yardstick*). That file will download to a default location, prob ably your Downloads folder. Your laptop made the initial decision of how to manage the file to meet your need of saving the image. It isn't always the best logical place to save the file, but it is the default setting. This initial decision is like the default dialect of your *Control Tactic* Acknowledgment Language.

The dialects are resisting, impressing, or sorting aspects of your experience. This sounds a bit vague but bear with me here. We are still looking at your personality at a higher triadic view, the seeds in the apple core, if you will, as opposed to your Enneagram Type. And your *Control Tactic* is just one seed in your core.

If you are Resisting-Dominant, you primarily manage your experience with a resistance to move or not move. It will depend on how much anger you feel in your body about the experience impacting your autonomy. Imagine the wasp is buzzing near you or landing on you. Even though you want to swat at it, you'll resist because you know it will make it angrier and more likely to sting you. Or, if your passion for the conservation of wasps kicks in, you'll resist the urge to tackle the person trying to kill the wasp. In both cases, that decision to resist would be protecting you from physical harm or impact.

If you are Impressing-Dominant, you primarily manage your experiences by impressing upon others for your own attention or significance. It might be an exaggeration or understatement, depending on how much shame you feel about how the experience is influencing your image or authenticity. Imagine someone knocks on the door to inquire about all the commotion. You'll show off your account of what happened, the role you played in "saving the day," or quietly make passive or dramatic moves like waving your arms to get attention, depending on the image you want to portray. The decision to make an impression to boost your significance is protecting you from rejection. In the wild, rejection means "left to die," so avoiding it is a survival instinct.

If you are Sorting-Dominant, you primarily manage your experience by sorting information into two general categories: safe or not safe. It might be efficient or unproductive sorting, depending on how much fear you feel about how the experience is affecting your own mental stability or security systems. When you see the wasp, your brain goes through your memories of what you know about wasps. You'll know it is probably assessing if you are a threat to it, so you'll leave it alone, or you'll take advantage of your authority and get rid of it. But if you are allergic to wasps, you'll not risk being around the wasp and will make sure your epi-pen isn't expired. By connecting the current experience to previous experiences or information, you are deciding (sorting) the priority of what will keep you the safest.

Everything you've read up to this point about your *Centers Reflex* has been an internal process. You received the stimulus of new information through your *Experience Gate* and found it significant enough (*Attention Filter*) to download it into your long-term memory (*Emotional Yardstick*). Now, your *Control Tactic* dialect tells your brain that you have decided to manage or control this new information.

Your *Control Tactic* is the internal trigger that now becomes the new stimulus for the external reactions of the *Stances Reflex* in the next chapter. Your *Stances Reflex* is your default executive function or how you externally react to meet your needs when you are on auto-pilot. It is your unconscious mind that controls the data processing in your brain. It isn't trying to be manipulative or deceitful, but to protect you using a tactic or strategy to respond to your experience in a way that has been hard-wired in your psyche.

Still, when you download that infographic on wasp stings to your laptop, the default location will pop up. But you still get to decide where to save it. You also get to decide to share it, duplicate it, or move it to the Trash. You are in control of how you ultimately manage your data, and likewise, your personality.

Before we move on to the rest of the traits of the *Stances Reflex*, let's take another look at the Enneagram stereotypes, this time armed with the knowledge of what's going on inside of their brains. How do the Acknowledgment Languages of the *Centers Reflexes* play out for each Enneagram Type?

The Centers Reflex is all internal, before you've had a chance to respond or react, and more importantly, before you've had an opportunity to adapt or conform to your nurtured personality.

Centers Reflex by Type

We've been looking at individual pieces of a lightning-fast reflexive process. Now the question is: How is that manifested within each Enneagram Type?

Remember, the *Centers Reflex* is all internal, before you have had a chance to respond or react, and more importantly, before you've had an opportunity to adapt or conform to your nurtured personality.

Just like using the numbers to refer to Enneagram Types to avoid using labels, I like to use the colors Red, Green, and Blue to refer to the collective traits of the first four languages of the 9AL™ that make up your *Centers Reflex*. This will remind you that the Moving Center, for example, isn't just about your body but also about impact, anger, and resisting, all working together to process your experiences.

Red = 8, 9, 1

Green = 2, 3, 4

Blue = 5, 6, 7

Even though the three types within each group have common traits, they are still very different personality types. The distinguishing features that make them different are:

1. Core Motivations, Strengths, and Mindsets

2. Innate Level of Consciousness of their own Personality: Aware / Unaware / Unaccepting

For each triad of the *Centers Reflexes*, one type is "Aware" of their personality traits, one is "Unaware," and one is "Unaccepting," as defined below:

Aware - Connected to and comfortable with expressing their Acknowledgment Languages dialects

Unaware - Out of touch with and uncomfortable expressing (represses) their dialects

Unaccepting - Aware of, but uncomfortable expressing (suppresses) their dialects

What does it mean to be a Red Type?

Center Reflex for Red Types (8, 9, 1)

1. Experience Gate - Body

2. Attention Filter - Impact

3. Emotional Yardstick - Anger

4. Control Tactic - Resisting

How they are the same:

All three of the types of the Moving Center experience their world through their Physical Intelligence (Body). Red Types struggle with reality's impact on their autonomy and carry resistance, tension, and anger in their bodies.

How they are different:

- **Type 8's** want to be strong, so they are aggressive and strong-willed but fear being controlled. They have a natural strength of "willpower." And they have a mindset to "overpower." (Aware)

- **Type 9's** want to be at ease, so they are "chill" and self-effacing but fear being disconnected. They have a natural ability to bring "harmony" or "togetherness." And they have a mindset of "inertia." (Unaware)

- **Type 1's** want to be proper, so they are principled and idealistic but fear being corrupted. They have a natural strength of "integrity." And they have a mindset of "restraint." (Unaccepting)

Let's say you are a **Type 8** who wants to be strong. Any impact on your body that makes you feel weak, like a wasp sting, would make you angry. Anger makes you feel powerful and gives you the energy of your strength and willpower. You are aware of when you are angry but also comfortable with it, aggressively seeking it out when you feel weak or controlled. You'll resist giving in to physical injury or boundary restrictions, toughing it out in order to feel in control of yourself, or overpowering others to feel in control of your environment.

However, if you are a **Type 9**, who wants to be at ease, you repress and lose touch with your anger. Your body feels the tension of being impacted, but your reflex is actively repressing the anger from your conscious awareness. Even though your anger gives you energy, like for a Type 8, your constant resistance to it drains you, and the repression weighs heavy in your body, leaving you with less energy than you believe you have. This gives you that "chill" appearance and the go-with-the-flow tendency to "borrow" energy from others, which fuels your inertia mindset or resistance to initiate change for yourself. So, your fear of disconnection is actually a fear of losing your source of energy, fusion. You'll resist conflict to maintain harmony, even if it means being self-effacing and flying under the radar.

If you are a **Type 1**, who wants to be proper, you are aware of your anger, unlike the Type 9, but show restraint when expressing it because it isn't proper. You're afraid of what it will lead to, namely the corruption of your morals or values. Your anger gives you the energy to pay attention to even the most minor details, especially in areas of improvement, always striving for the ideal principles of your code of ethics. The suppression of anger impacts your body with tension, giving you a rigid or stiff posture, and having difficulty relaxing. This leads to a lot of tension build-up and can manifest as physical disorders.

What does it mean to be a Green Type?

Center Reflex for Green Types (2, 3, 4)

1. Experience Gate - Heart

2. Attention Filter - Image

3. Emotional Yardstick - Shame

4. Control Tactic - Impressing

How they are the same:

All three of the types of the Feeling Center experience their world through their Emotional Intelligence (Heart). Green Types struggle with their self-image or identity and respond with exaggeration and shame about their authenticity and significance.

How they are different:

- **Type 2's** want to be appreciated, so they are generous and seductive but fear being seen as needy. They have a natural ability to "nurture." And they have a mindset of "flattery." (Aware)

- **Type 3's** want to be admired, so they are ambitious and status-conscious but fear being seen as an imposter. They have a natural strength for "self-assurance." And they have a mindset to "compete." (Unaware)

- **Type 4's** want to be different, so they are mysterious and emotionally authentic but fear not being seen as original. They have a natural ability to "endure." And they have a mindset of "melancholy." (Unaccepting)

As a **Type 2**, who wants to be appreciated, you want to maintain an image of availability to others, like a mother with her newborn ready to meet all of his needs. In this way, you are attuned to the needs of others, particularly emotional needs of significance. You are generous with your time and energy conducting acts of service and reassuring or encouraging others with compliments and gratitude. You are aware of your own needs, but tending to your needs means you are less available to tend to others. To get around the shame of seeing yourself as selfish or needy, you might impose or impress your needs onto others, hoping they will reciprocate as a token of their appreciation. You might even exaggerate your care-taking load to indirectly ask for help, or seduce others with flattery to persuade them to take care of your needs of their own volition.

If you are a **Type 3**, who wants to be admired, you want to be in the spotlight and be seen as the best of the best. You repress your shame like the Type 9s repress anger, which gives you that "shameless" and self-assured confidence that people look up to. Unaware and uncomfortable with your self-image of not doing enough or being a loser or failure, you are driven to win at everything you attempt, even if it means cutting corners, taking advantage, or exaggerating your abilities or accomplishments to impress others about your status and significance. You tend to change your image based on the social circle you're in at the time in order to receive the kind of attention or admiration you want from them. This social shape-shifting feeds your repressed shame of being "found out" or seen as a fake and can leak out in emotional outbursts or withdrawal in embarrassment.

Being a **Type 4**, who wants to be different, you adopt the image that will make you stand out in the crowd as a unique individual, constantly comparing to avoid the shame of copying or being a "sheep." You experience people as emotions and emotions as facts. However, you actively suppress expressing your emotions directly because you fear they won't be validated in the way you romanticize it. You are almost ashamed of being happy because it doesn't feel genuine. That leaves you with a melancholic demeanor which feels more authentic to you. You seek to impress others with mysterious and deeply meaningful symbols of the past sufferings you've endured, most often through your style or creations. When their significance is lost on people, you feel misunderstood and ashamed about your own significance.

What does it mean to be a Blue Type?

Center Reflex for Blue Types (5, 6, 7)

1. Experience Gate - Mind

2. Attention Filter - Safety

3. Emotional Yardstick - Fear

4. Control Tactic - Sorting

How they are the same:

All three of the types of the Thinking Center experiences are in their Mental Intelligence (Mind). Blue Types struggle with organizing their thoughts about their safety, security, or access to support, causing fear or anxiety about their stability.

How are they different:

- **Type 5's** want to be factual, so they observe and collect data but fear being depleted. They have the natural strength of "honesty." And they have a mindset to "detach." (Aware)

- **Type 6's** want to be supported, so they advocate and make systems but fear being unprepared. They have a natural strength of "dependability." And they have a mindset of "doubt." (Unaware)

- **Type 7's** want to be content, so they are indulgent and optimistic but fear being deprived. They have a natural ability for "immersion." And they have a mindset to "explore." (Unaccepting)

As a **Type 5**, who wants to be factual, you first sort incoming information as true or false. You are a collector of knowledge, resources, or skills to ensure you will be capable of participating in a conversation or event without the fear of feeling ignorant or not understanding what is expected of you. You are aware and comfortable with the safety of not participating and only observing from the outside, and of being completely honest, especially if others are misinformed. You feel the need to detach physically and emotionally to be able to process or sort all the information into the interesting and unusual categories and connections of your inner thought world. Else, you are afraid any intrusions will drain your energy and leave you feeling depleted, even though you have more energy than you believe you do.

If you are a **Type 6**, who wants to be supported, you first sort incoming information into the categories of trust or doubt. You repress your fears of instability and actively identify worst-case scenarios in order to create a plan for each case. That way you feel prepared for anything that might possibly threaten you. Your repressed fear manifests as a hypervigilant need to look for the threats you might have overlooked. You are an advocate for supporting others' points of view, or the devil's advocate to test ideas or beliefs for their validity. Because people have differing ideas of what they consider threats, you can get overwhelmed with all of the possibilities and have a hard time making decisions or prioritizing. You are constantly creating systems that you can depend on to help you "think" less and have more peace of mind, but you're constantly tweaking them as new information arrives.

Now let's say you are a **Type 7** who wants to be content. You crave experiences that are fun, exciting, creative, novel, and indulgent. You sort incoming ideas and thoughts into what you believe will be positive or negative experiences. You are aware of your fears and insecurities. However, since those lead to negative experiences, you suppress them by getting immersed in your positive experiences to drown out negative thoughts, escaping them by exploring rabbit trails of ideas, or reframing them with relentless optimism. You don't like feeling deprived of opportunities or having limited options, which actually stems from a fear of being bored and discontent. If you sit still, you are left alone with your thoughts, and all those suppressed insecurities begin to flood you. So, you seek stimulation by finding creative ways to cheer yourself up or entertain yourself with the resources you do have.

10

Understanding Your External Response as a Reflex of Your Enneagram Type

Every year before the pandemic, my family and I would travel to Nashville, TN, for Terry's favorite race called The Flying Monkey Marathon. It's hours of hills, trails, and grass, but he is a glutton for pain, I guess, and he runs it every year. The first year he participated in it I was homeschooling the kids, and we loved making a field trip out of anything. So I planned for places to go while we waited for Dad to finish his race. I sat in front of my laptop and thought, I wonder how far the Children's

Museum is. So, I Googled "Children's museums in Nashville," and it came up showing its location on the map.

I love comparing the Enneagram to a roadmap and GPS system. It gauges where you are, where you're going if you've missed a turn, and how to reroute yourself when you get lost. When you say to Siri "Directions to the Children's Museum," it needs to know three things:

- Your position - What is your current point A?
- Your orientation - What direction are you headed?
- Your speed - How fast are you traveling?

With this information, Siri will be able to tell you how far you are from point B, whether you need to make a U-turn, and calculate an estimated time of arrival based on your speed.

Stances fit nicely into this visual. Your Core Type's Stance is your default posture or attitude about how you get your needs met. It is a reflex triggered by your *Centers Reflex's* decision (*Control Tactic*) to manage the new information you've been internally processing. Your *Stances Reflex* has now kicked in and must be carried out to completion.

Stances Reflex

The Enneagram Stances are based on Karen Horney's Psychoanalytic Social Theory that she developed to describe ten neurotic needs people use as excessive defense mechanisms, as outlined in her book *Self-Analysis*. No one really uses the word neurosis anymore, but in 1942 when the book was published, neurosis was the general term to describe drastic or irrational behaviors that manifest as a mental health illness, namely anxiety disorders. Her theory is strictly a social theory, addressing the adaptive behaviors (the learned or nurtured part of your personality) of dealing with not getting your ultimate needs met for safety and comfort.

Horney classified her ten neurotic needs into three categories: Withdrawn, Aggressive, Dependent. These three labels were adopted as the Stances of the Enneagram. Unlike Horney's theory which describes the neurotic fixations that can lead to personality disorders, your Enneagram Stance is a part of your natural temperament. This is an important distinction for understanding the normal default for your personality's self-protection reflex.

When I was planning our trip to Nashville and clicked to see the directions to the Children's Museum, the default location is where I currently was at the time, which was at home. But I needed the directions from the race's finish line, not my house. The Maps app is wired or programmed to automatically assign your current location as your point A, just like your brain is wired or programmed to assign your default Stance. It just takes a few clicks to adjust point A to get a more accurate, more efficient and helpful set of directions for reaching your destination. But you would never give the app a 1-star rating because of this — there is nothing wrong with the app. It's functioning according to its design, even if the default settings weren't appropriate for my current intentions.

In this chapter, I want to address this more neutral view of your Enneagram Stance that is not an indication of mental illness but of your normal wiring or nature of your personality. Once you recognize that you just need rerouting, you can simply take steps to do that without self-judgment.

Like the *Centers Reflex*, each triad grouping of your *Stances Reflex* has its own package of traits. The following list is the last five languages of the 9AL™ — three languages that identify your type's social position, speed, and orientation, and two languages that identify the blind spots of your Stance.

5.   Social Style (position)

6.   Pace Style (speed)

7.   Timeline Focus (orientation)

8.   Timeline Blind Spot

9.   Centers Blind Spot

Let's review the descriptions of the Stances and the color labels I've assigned them to represent the collective traits listed above.

Withdrawn Stance = you move away from people to get your needs met. These are the "Cyan" Types 9, 4, and 5.

Aggressive Stance = you move against people to get your needs met. These are the "Magenta" Types 8, 3, and 7.

Dependent Stance = you move towards people to get your needs met. These are the "Yellow" Types 1, 2, and 6.

When your *Stances Reflex* is triggered, all five languages speak within a fraction of a second of each other. Still, we will look at each of them individually so you can understand the role each one serves in your external processing of getting your needs met.

Even though your Core Type's Stance represents average behaviors, meaning they are neither healthy nor unhealthy, when you are under stress, these behaviors could be red flags of unhealthy behaviors on the horizon. More on that in Chapter 11 on Blind Spots. For that reason, I'm including how a person speaking each dialect might appear to others, which can create an *Experience Gap* by making assumptions or judgments about your perceived intentions.

Social Style

Your *Social Style* language is how you socially position yourself in respect to other people in order to get your needs met. This is your normal default style, not your style under stress or security.

If you are Avoiding-Dominant, you unconsciously want to meet your needs independently. It could be a desire for self-sufficiency, personal competency, self-preservation, or minimizing distractions that drives you to avoid people. You unconsciously believe you need to spend all of your energy focused inward to protect your ability to process information and respond effectively. You might appear cold, aloof, reserved, or odd to others.

If you are Confronting-Dominant, you unconsciously want to be challenged to meet your needs. It could mean delegating, debating, competing, or exploiting to get that "push back" that motivates you. You want to meet your needs independently, but you unconsciously believe you need an opponent in order to process information and respond efficiently. You might appear argumentative, overwhelming, confident, or pushy to others.

If you are Abiding-Dominant, you unconsciously want acceptance for meeting your needs. It could be conforming to social expectations, putting others' needs before your own, or seeking out an authority to follow or partner with. You unconsciously believe you need someone's approval in order to process information and respond appropriately. You might appear accommodating, submissive, friendly, or strict to others.

You will speak all three dialects depending on your stress and health levels, but one will be the one that comes most immediately to you when you aren't thinking about your own behaviors, but naturally being yourself.

Pace Style

Your *Pace Style* language is your temperament's processing speed or the pace that you unconsciously believe will produce the best environment for meeting your needs.

If you are Slow-Paced, you primarily want to process information and respond gradually, gently, and in a measured way. To others, this might look like shutting down, maybe with a "deer in headlights" look, but you really just need the space to detach from others so you can slow down and be intentional. You might be described as slowpoke, lazy, deliberate, or dismissive.

If you are Fast-Paced, you primarily want to process information and respond immediately. To others, you might look impulsive, but you just talk fast, think quickly, or take action right away so you can move on to the next thing. You might be described as being reckless, erratic, spontaneous, or abrupt.

If you are Compliant-Paced, you primarily want to process information and respond cooperatively. To others, you might look like you're wavering or being a pushover, but you really just want to create a collaborative environment. You might be described as obliging, yielding, adaptable, or permissive.

Timeline Focus

Timeline Focus is your orientation to the Past, Present, and Future timeframes to give context to the information you are processing.

If you are Past-Referencing, you primarily view the past as the facts to give context to the present. To you, the past is the primary predictor of the future. You don't expect much to change without there first being past evidence of the need for change. That change is also typically seen as temporary; therefore, you will revert to your past ways once the need for the temporary change has abated. This feels safe and predictable. To others, you might look like a historian, nostalgic, stubborn, and slow to change, avoiding the inevitable as long as you can.

If you are Future-Referencing, you primarily view the future possibilities as facts to give context to the present. To you, change is exciting, and you expect everything to change for the better. More of the same either feels boring, chaotic, or passive. To others, you might look like a visionary, multipotentialite, ambitious, unrealistic or impractical like a dreamer with your head in the clouds.

If you are Present-Referencing, you primarily view the present as the only facts. To you, the moment of the current experience is what matters. This creates a state of flux between what was and what could be, resulting in indecisiveness and inconsistency. To others, you might look observant, forgiving, on guard, or vacillating between different opinions or actions.

Blind Spots

The last two languages are like a secret language of yours, like writing a note with invisible ink that even you can't read.

Your blind spots could be literal blind spots, like when driving a car. Have you ever parked your car in a space and accidentally scraped your front bumper on the concrete? You don't know it has happened until you hear that jaw-clenching grinding noise, as the undercarriage of your car meets the curbside. And the only fix is to backup and prepare to go through that face-contorting experience again in order to set things right.

However, your blind spots might be a distraction. It could be an area that you intently focus on but are blind to the unproductivity or ineffectuality of your overall efforts. Have you ever been so focused on your rear backup camera in a garage that you accidentally knocked the side-view mirror on a pole?

You are not connected to your blind spots by default. First, it takes effort to be aware of them. Then, it takes effort to intentionally look at them. Again, these blind spots of your Stance are a part of your wiring and nature. Below, I'm describing your initial unconscious impulses and not how you've adapted as you've either matured or disintegrated.

Timeline Blind Spot

This blind spot is closely related to your *Timeline Focus* or which timeframe you reference or orient yourself toward. If you're in a car on a road trip, being Past-Referencing is facing the back window looking at everything you've passed. Or, if you're the driver, it's always looking back in the rearview mirror to see where you've been. The Future-Referencing is looking ahead and anticipating what you need to do to get to where you are going. Inside of the car represents the Present-Referencing. You could be engaged by looking both forward and backward, or you could be distracted by the music, conversation, a nap, fully trusting the driver (or auto-driver) to get you where you need to go.

If you are Present-Blind, you are also Past-Referencing. You like to retreat to the past to get your truth. Sometimes your past might be a fantasy or a romanticized past, but it serves as evidence of what works and what doesn't work when trying to meet your needs. You'll unconsciously spend your energy preparing for a future that aligns with your past choices, even if you consciously want to change. You will unconsciously be blind to the details of what you should do NOW or "in the car" to create the future you really want.

If you are Past-Blind, you are also Future-Referencing. You like to stay ahead of the game and are open to new ways to meet your needs. You'll unconsciously forget to look in the rearview mirror and spend your energy creating your future, which can be a fantasized or romanticized future. You will unconsciously be blind to the details of lessons you have already learned (or should have learned) in the past that could better inform you on what you should do NOW that is more realistic and practical.

If you are Future-Blind, you are also Present-Referencing. Concerned mostly with what is going on "in the car," you might miss your turn because you weren't paying attention to what was ahead, or you might spend your energy accommodating stop requests without considering the future impact on your road trip plans. You will unconsciously be blind to the details of future consequences of your present actions because you were focused on creating or making the most of the moment.

Centers Blind Spot

This blind spot is closely related to your primary Centers of Intelligence: Moving, Feeling, and Thinking. Of the three types within a Center Triad, one type will be Action-Blind, one type will be Emotional-Blind, and one type will be Thought-Blind. This is a simple way to be able to distinguish the types sharing the same *Centers Reflex* or internal brain processing of new information.

If you are Action-Blind, you are inactive or slow to move into action because you are busy processing your thoughts and emotions. Or, you will unconsciously move into action without fully processing your thoughts or feelings, making your actions unproductive and out of alignment with your ideas and your emotions.

If you are Emotional-Blind, you ignore or are quick to bypass vulnerable emotions so you can process your thoughts and to-do lists. Or, you will unconsciously focus too much on your emotions, allowing them to overwhelm your thoughts and actions, making your emotions unproductive and out of alignment with your beliefs and what you want to achieve.

If you are Thought-Blind, you are out of touch with your thoughts, preoccupied with processing your emotions or acting on your tasks. Or, you will unconsciously overthink your emotions or actions, making your thoughts unproductive and out of alignment with how you feel and what you want to accomplish.

For Types 9, 3, and 6, this blind spot might be confusing. Type 9's are in the moving center but are also Action-Blind. Type 3's are in the feeling center but are also Emotional-Blind. Type 6's are in the thinking center but are also Thought-Blind. So if you went through the traits of the *Centers Reflexes* (first four of the

9AL™) and felt like you were split among many of the dialects, this blind spot could be the reason why. Most Type 9's believe they are "thinkers" over being "doers." Most Type 6's identify as "feelers" over being "thinkers." And, most Type 3's consider themselves "doers" rather than "feelers."

More on blind spots in Chapter 11, but before we jump ahead, let's go through each of the stereotypes of the Enneagram to illustrate the differences within each triad group.

"You are not connected to your blind spots by default. First, it takes effort to be aware of them. Then, it takes effort to intentionally look at them."

Stances Reflex by Type

We've been breaking down the split-second process of your *Personality Reflexes*. Using the color labels Cyan, Magenta, and Yellow to refer to the collective traits that make up your *Stances Reflex*, let's look at how each Enneagram Type tends to behave by default. Remember, your personality's self-protection reflexes occur before you have had a chance to adjust to your nurtured personality.

Cyan = 9, 4, 5

Magenta = 8, 3, 7

Yellow = 1, 2, 6

Even though each group of three types has these traits in common, they are very different personality types for the same reasons as the *Centers Reflex*. Each has its own core motivations, strengths, and mindsets. Within a triad group, exactly one type will be "Aware," "Unaware," and "Unaccepting." Refer back to Chapter 9 to remind you of the definitions of what that means.

Additionally, within a triad group, exactly one type will be "Red," "Green," and "Blue."

What does it mean to be a Cyan Type?

Stance Reflex for Cyan Types (9, 4, 5)

5.   Social Style - Avoiding

6.   Pace Style - Slow

7.   Timeline Focus - Past-Referencing

8.   Timeline Blind Spot - Present-Blind

9.   Centers Blind Spot - Action-Blind

How are they the same:

All three of the types of Withdrawn Stance move away or avoid people to get their needs met. This allows them to slow down and refer to the past to process their thoughts and feelings before taking action. If unaware of their blind spots, this can take too long, and they might miss their moment of opportunity or choose actions that are often unproductive.

How they are different:

- **Type 9's** want to be at ease, so they are "chill" and self-effacing but fear being disconnected. They have a natural ability to bring "harmony" or "togetherness." And they have a mindset of "inertia." (Unaware / Red)

- **Type 4's** want to be different, so they are mysterious and emotionally authentic but fear not being seen as original. They have a natural ability to "endure." And they have a mindset of "melancholy." (Unaccepting / Green)

- **Type 5's** want to be factual, so they observe and collect data but fear being depleted. They have the natural strength of "honesty." And they have a mindset to "detach." (Aware / Blue)

Type 9 is the Red Type of the Cyan Types, meaning their red traits (Body, Impact, Anger, Resisting) trigger them to take a Withdrawn Stance in order to be at ease — "resisting" moving their own bodies in order to "go with the flow." If you are a Type 9 and your wife asks on your road trip, "Where do you want to stop to eat?" you might be slow to answer while you process which places in the past have caused a conflict of interest so that you can avoid suggesting those. With your strength of "togetherness" and "inertia" mindset, you will likely happily settle for what everyone else wants, withdrawing from your personal wants, needs, or opinions to avoid a disconnection with others.

Type 4 is the Green Type of the Cyan Types, meaning they withdraw as a result of their green traits (Heart, Image, Shame, Impressing). If you are a Type 4, you like to withdraw "in plain sight" in order to still be seen, impressing people with your endurance for suffering. You will reference the past to help you make a decision and slow down to relive the emotional impact your past experiences have made on you. With your strength to "endure" and "melancholy" mindset, you will long for a rescuer to accept and appreciate your uniqueness. You often withdraw from your dreams of happiness and become unproductive.

Type 5 is the Blue Type of the Cyan Types, meaning their blue traits (Mind, Security, Fear, Sorting) trigger their stance to withdraw to sort their priorities so that they can conserve their resources. As a Type 5, you will scan your memory to discern if you have enough past information to add that will make a conversation or experience interesting. If not, you won't feel the need to spend the extra energy to participate. But if you have a fun fact emerge from your data bank in your brain, you might feel compelled to share it, even if it sends the conversation down a rabbit trail and keeps you from doing productive tasks. With your, sometimes brutal, "honesty" and "detached" mindset, you set narrow boundaries in your life to fend people off and restrict your activity.

What does it mean to be a Magenta Type?

Stance Reflex for Magenta Types (8, 3, 7)

5. Social Style - Confronting

6. Pace Style - Fast

7. Timeline Focus - Future-referencing

8. Timeline Blind Spot - Past-blind

9. Centers Blind Spot - Emotional-blind

How are they the same:

All three types of the Aggressive Stance move against or confront people to get their needs met. This allows them to expedite the process so they can keep moving forward with actions toward their ideas for the future. If they are unaware of their blind spots, unresolved past issues will slow them down. They move impulsively, unconsciously acting on unproductive emotions of anger, shame, or fear.

How they are different:

*   **Type 8's** want to be strong, so they are aggressive and strong-willed but fear being controlled. They have a natural strength of "willpower." And they have a mindset to "overpower." (Aware / Red)

*   **Type 3's** want to be admired, so they are ambitious and status-conscious but fear being seen as an imposter. They

have a natural strength for "self-assurance." And they have a mindset to "compete." (Unaware / Green)

- **Type 7's** want to be content, so they are indulgent and optimistic but fear being deprived. They have a natural ability for "immersion." And they have a mindset to "explore." (Unaccepting / Blue)

Type 8 is the Red Type of the Magenta Types, meaning their red traits (Body, Impact, Anger, Resisting) trigger their Aggressive Stance, resisting inaction by overpowering others. If you are a Type 8, you might become domineering or intimidating when confronting others to avoid being controlled. You reference a chaotic or unjust future that you must bring into order as soon as possible, protecting what or who you feel deserves your protection and eliminating the rest. With your strength of sheer "willpower" and "overpower" mindset, you only allow emotional pain to make you stronger, and you leave the past in the past.

Type 3 is the Green Type of the Magenta Types, meaning they take an Aggressive Stance due to their green traits (Heart, Image, Shame, Impressing) to impress others with their status. If you are a Type 3, you confront others in order to discern how you compare to them. It might push you to be better or give you an opportunity to present the image that you believe they will admire, especially about what you've been able to achieve in a short amount of time. With your "self-assurance" and "competitive" mindset, you don't have time for emotions because you believe emotions are embarrassing traits that hold you back from the finish line.

Type 7 is the Blue Type of the Magenta Types, meaning their blue traits (Mind, Security, Fear, Sorting) trigger their Aggressive Stance to sort out the negative parts of their life and be an aggressive optimist. If you are a Type 7, you feel trapped by negative or vulnerable emotions, which inhibits your ability to carry out your plans; therefore, you never fully feel the pain of your past. With your strength for "immersion" and "explore" mindset, you are constantly pursuing your future happiness through experiences that give you new knowledge, new perspectives, and new possibilities to think about.

What does it mean to be a Yellow Type?

Stance Reflex for Yellow Types (1, 2, 6)

5. Social Style - Abiding

6. Pace Style - Compliant

7. Timeline Focus - Present-referencing

8. Timeline Blind Spot - Future-blind

9. Centers Blind Spot - Thought-blind

How are they the same:

All three of the Types of the Dependent Stance move toward or with people to get their needs met. This allows them to fluctuate their pace in order to comply with the demands of the present moment. If unaware of their blind spots, they can lose track of their own thoughts and prevent their ability to have an independent future.

How they are different:

*   **Type 1's** want to be proper, so they are principled and idealistic but fear being corrupted. They have a natural strength of "integrity." And they have a mindset of "restraint." (Unaccepting / Red)

*   **Type 2's** want to be appreciated, so they are generous and seductive but fear being seen as needy. They have a natural ability to "nurture." And they have a mindset of "flattery." (Aware / Green)

- **Type 6's** want to be supported, so they advocate and make systems but fear being unprepared. They have a natural strength of "dependability." And they have a mindset of "doubt." (Unaware / Blue)

Type 1 is the Red Type of the Yellow Types, meaning their Dependent Stance is triggered by their red traits (Body, Impact, Anger, Resisting), resisting your anger by showing restraint in the current moment, depending on how proper you sense it is to show your anger. If you are a Type 1, you abide by what the moment calls you to do, in other words, what you should do. With your strength of "integrity," you restrain from what you really want to do or say in the present in order to be aligned with an idealized future. You have high standards for yourself and those around you and expect compliance with them. When you and everyone inevitably fall short, your thoughts become critical and unproductive.

Type 2 is the Green Type of the Yellow Types, meaning they take a Dependent Stance due to their green traits (Heart, Image, Shame, Impressing) to impress others with their generosity and attentiveness. If you are a Type 2, you depend on others to give you what you need because you don't want to be seen as selfish. You find ways to "Do unto others as you would have them do unto you," foreseeing reciprocity from others, and are deeply hurt and unappreciated when they don't. With your strength to "nurture" and "flattery" mindset, you will cheerfully continue to accommodate the physical and emotional needs of others, displaying yourself as a martyred matriarch, and unproductively thinking you know what's best for them.

Type 6 is the Blue Type of the Yellow Types, meaning their blue traits (Mind, Security, Fear, Sorting) trigger their Dependent Stance to seek out other people's perspectives before deciding if you trust them or if you trust your own perspective. If you are a Type 6, you will ask questions or make statements about your certainty of what is currently happening and what that means for the certainty of the future. Your compliance with differing opinions and perspectives can cause you to waver. With your strength of "dependability" and "doubt" mindset, you are prepared for the worst-case scenarios and create support systems for people, including decision-making processes so you won't get lost in overthinking.

The descriptions of each type in both this and the previous chapter are unconscious parts of your Enneagram's Core Type. They are automatic and are neither healthy nor unhealthy at face value. When you use the description of the *Stances Reflexes* together with the description of the *Centers Reflexes*, you'll be well equipped to start your process of elimination to verify your Core Type. If you do not know your type yet, remember to look at the motivations, not behaviors, of when you were a child, a young independent, and your current age. Be as objective as possible without giving in to the tendency to view yourself as your "idealized self," a part of Karen Horney's mature theory of neurosis. Neurosis is a distorted way of looking at the world and oneself through a narrow window of your box. This is the bottom of the ladder, but it is NOT your automatic, natural way of being.

Sometimes your blind spots take you down a notch. But you also have blind spots that mask how perfect and powerful you truly are, and they hold you back. In the next chapter, I'll revisit the symbols and infrastructure of the Enneagram to show you where to look for the validating (and humbling) pieces of your personality that can turn stumbling blocks into stepping stones.

11

UNDERSTANDING YOUR BLIND SPOTS

When my Enneagram mentor helped me identify myself as Type 7, I was a little shell-shocked. In theory, I couldn't be another type. I checked all of the proverbial boxes for the motivations and stress patterns for Type 7. I thought to myself, "But I'm not fun. And I'm an introvert. And I'm waaaaay too responsible to be a Type 7."

I certainly had some misconception blind spots about what it means to be a Type 7, and I also had blind spots about how I saw myself. This "false self " or "idealized self " view I had was holding me back from being my best self.

According to both Abraham Maslow's hierarchy of needs and Karen Horney's mature theory of neurosis, Self-Actualization is the ultimate need all people strive to meet, meaning the "core of one's own being and potential." Horney added that we all have two views of ourselves by distinguishing: the real self and the ideal self. Your real self is your true, authentic, and original self. Your ideal self can be a pseudo self or persona: a façade, defense, or a mask between your real self and the world. It's the appearance of being real but lacking depth or feeling empty on the inside. Horney believed that you wouldn't be free to realize your full purpose until you have an accurate sense of your own true self.

The *Ladder of Awareness* inside your box can give you this accurate sense of your true self. The top of your ladder is your real self, your healthy self, able to rise above your personality. At the bottom of your ladder, when you are stuck inside of your box with only a limited or distorted view, is your false self.

Notice the middle of the ladder, where your average behaviors are. It is not outside of the box, but it also isn't within the view of the window. When you are on auto-pilot, these are the behaviors you default to when you aren't thinking about your personality. Again, these are neither healthy nor unhealthy. Still, they can be a blind spot if you're not intentionally climbing up the ladder to look out of the box or descending down to look out the window. If you notice an *Experience Gap*, it could be due to this average behavior space on the ladder.

Now that I've been proudly wearing my Type 7 cape for a few years now, it is much easier for me to look back and see precise moments of being both past-blind and emotional-blind. It is almost comical how obvious Type 7 is the correct profile for me and that I was blind to it. I didn't remember the wee Jen that was the "life of the party" as the youngest of three siblings, telling silly jokes, singing made-up lyrics, bouncing off the walls, complaining of being bored, jabbering your ears off, dancing, more singing, more dancing, and more jabbering. I had allowed unprocessed negative emotions to cloud my vision. I didn't see myself as sad or depressed. Those are negative and emotions: yuck and yuck. Instead, I saw myself as boring, an image I still struggle with if I'm not intentional to catch that red flag.

Your blind spots are not the red flag. Just like you will probably never see your own spleen (unless you are intentional about it), you won't see your blind spots if you don't go looking for them. Ideally, you'd be in the habit of looking for them, in the same way you immediately check your side-view mirrors before you change lanes on the highway. If you don't, you might sideswipe another vehicle. You don't want to wait for a red flag like that to warn you. It's kind of too late.

Wouldn't it be nice if the other driver saw you coming, predicted you didn't see him, and honked his horn to alert you that he was in your blind spot?

Good news! The Enneagram has a red flag warning just like that friendly driver. It's called your Stress Number. When you are headed down your Stress Path toward your Stress Number, beginning to behave like the stereotypes of that number, the Enneagram gives a little "toot toot" to get your attention that you are on your Stress Path.

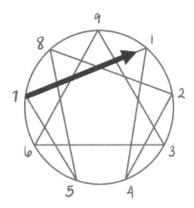

As a Type 7, my Stress Number is Type 1. So, when I start to notice that I am beginning to become principled or idealistic, becoming angry or critical, that is my red flag that I'm under stress. This means the extension ladder has been retracted, and the lid to my box has been shut. My only option for seeing what is going on out there seems to be to climb down the ladder, look out of the window, and see the distorted view of my boring self, trapped by motherhood, special diets, and the failures at adulting. My impulsiveness is no longer as benign as an act of stopping in the middle of a sentence to blurt out the punchline to the joke I forgot. Instead, it might turn into a shopping spree, overindulging on a tv series, or another manic attempt to escape the anxiety of life. This is called Disintegration.

The top of the ladder is another one of your blind spots. It's there, but it can't be seen.

When I'm too busy looking out the "Everything is not that awesome" window, I'm completely unaware that the lid is even closed.

However, if I notice the red flag of my Stress Number's behaviors, I'll remember to look up instead. "Oh yeah, that lid opens, and this ladder extends!" Now I have the option to climb up the ladder where I can see my real self, optimistic, practical, and accomplished.

The day I got lost in Athens, Greece, looking for the Acropolis, was the first time I had explored a foreign city all by myself. With only a (useless) map and a few Greek coins for the metro, I left my sister at the hostel who decided to do laundry, which relieved me from carrying the backpack with me. (I'm not a chump to leave her behind, she'd already been to the Acropolis.) I probably walked around in circles for at least an hour, hiding behind doors to study the map to try to translate the road signs. I didn't want to make it totally obvious I was a lost tourist. I was so stressed and mad at myself that I had come "all this way" and had already wasted so much time. I decided to suck it up and ask someone. I let out an exasperated groan and threw my head back in defeat... and there it was, upon the mountain in all of its ginormous glory, mocking me as if to say, "I was up here the entire time, you doofus." If I hadn't limited myself to a street-level view, I would have already been up there by now!

This was my Type 7's stress pattern, and each type has its own unique red flag to remind them to look up.

You can also use the 9AL™ or the mindsets to recognize your Stress Number's behaviors. For example:

> If you are a **Type 8**, you might be under stress if you are withdrawing and avoiding people to conserve your resources like your Stress Number Type 5.

> If you are a **Type 9** who begins to overthink threats and conflicts like your Stress Number Type 6, you might want to stop and open the hatch.

> In the same manner,
> - if you are a **Type 1** who gets a bit melancholic about the state of your existence like a Type 4;
> - if you are a **Type 2** who becomes aggressive or controlling like a Type 8;
> - if you are a **Type 3** who becomes unmotivated and withdraws like a Type 9;
> - if you are a **Type 4** who seeks out people to rescue like a Type 2;
> - if you are a **Type 5** who becomes indulgent or impulsive like a Type 7; or
> - if you are a **Type 6** who becomes overly ambitious to impress others like a Type 3.

Core Number	Stress Number	Security Number
8	5	2
9	6	3
1	4	7
2	8	4
3	9	6
4	2	1
5	7	8
6	3	9
7	1	5

When you choose to open the lid of your box, extend the ladder out, and begin to climb it, you'll start behaving like your Security Number's healthy behaviors the higher you climb.

Your Security Path follows the other line or arrow coming from your Core Type, which points to your Security Number. (For me as a Type 7, my Security Number is Type 5.) It is also your Growth Path which, when followed, is called Integration, closing the gap between your real self and ideal self.

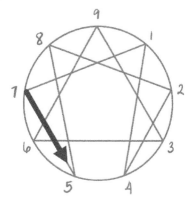

However, your Security Path is not always the same as your Growth Path. Contrary to what most recreational Enneagram enthusiasts believe, Security does not equal Growth and Newsflash... Stress does not mean automatic Disintegration. There are two different continuums of your Core Type: Stress to Security and Unhealthy to Healthy. Being able to have a clear mental image of this will be key to establishing and enforcing healthy boundaries for yourself.

Remember the composite symbol of your box, with your ladder inside and balanced on your *Personality Tripod.* And also remember that each person has their own individual box with their own ladder template based on their own Core Type.

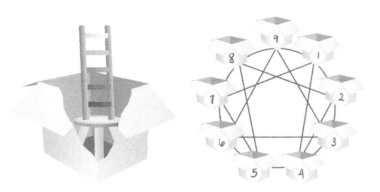

If you look at the diagram like a roadmap with your box as the "You are Here" symbol on your GPS navigation system, your Stress-to-Security continuum tells you where your box is on the map. Are you at "Home" at your Core Type's position? Or are you on the path to a different number? You have access to all of them! Remember, the diagram is a microcosm of your psyche, essence, core, and wholeness. You could be traveling to your Stress Number, Security Number, a Wing, or a style, like your leadership style or attachment style. You are so dynamic and capable of adapting to your environment.

The Unhealthy-to-Healthy continuum tells you where you are on the ladder. So even if you are on your Security Path, you could be bebopping along looking through the small window at a distorted view of your security. Or you might be on a middle rung of the ladder still within your box on cruise control while you relax.

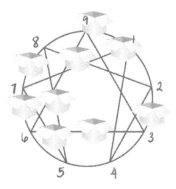

For me, as a Type 7 with a Type 5 Security Number, it might look like the difference between isolating myself to read in order to study and grow (healthy) vs. to escape anxiety (unhealthy) or to pass the time because I'm bored (average). Your average to unhealthy responses while on your Security Path might give you a false sense of Security and lead you to believe you are being healthy, just because no sirens are going off. This is still a false self image and another blind spot to be aware of.

Likewise, if you are on your Stress Path, It doesn't insinuate that you're stuck inside of the box. The worst-case scenario is being on your Stress Path at the bottom of your ladder, meaning you are not healthily responding to your stress and only have a distorted view of your reality. This takes you further away from your real self. But not all stress is bad stress. There is also good stress, called *eustress*, that has beneficial effects on your motivations, emotional well-being, and performance. When your Stress Path's red flag honks at you, you have a choice to climb or descend. When you look up and ascend, that's a healthy response on your Stress Path! It's like sticking your head out the sunroof as you head toward your Stress Number, staring it dead in the face and yelling, "Let's do this!"

Empowering to know you have that option, isn't it?

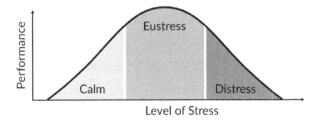

As a Type 7 with a Type 1 Stress Number, I might be choosing to take on a tedious task knowing that it is the responsible thing to do in order to have a more meaningful experience in the future. Like, planning the details of the Race Day schedule in Nashville: making sure Terry gets to the starting line on time, the kids have the right snacks according to their special diets, directions and estimated driving times for excursions, alternative plans in case of meltdowns, and returning to the finish line to see Terry cross it. Even though it was stressful for me to implement so much structure into our day, I was able to turn it into eustress and perform the task well to ensure it was a fun day.

Let's get a visual of the blind spots these two continuums show you. Imagine each number on the Enneagram is a stop on the map and represents a *Library of Behaviors*. These are the ladder "templates" of each Core Type. As you travel around the map and stop at the libraries, you can borrow behaviors like borrowing books from your local library. When you reach for a book and check it out, you don't become that number; you simply behave like the number. The ladder inside of your box grounds you to your own unique personality's perspective, meaning even though you've borrowed another type's behaviors, your *Personality Paintbrush* will still be biased toward your own motivations, strengths, and mindset.

Each ladder template is like a bookshelf with nine shelves, matching up with the nine Levels of Health, or nine rungs, where the topmost shelf holds the healthiest behavior "books" for that number. Where you are on your own ladder inside of your box determines which behaviors you can reach when visiting other libraries. If you are on a middle rung of your own ladder, approaching your Security Number's library, you can only access its middle rung of behaviors (or middle shelf of books). The higher you reach, the higher you can climb your own ladder. The higher you climb, the higher shelves you can reach. However, you never swap ladders or change numbers (remember Rule #2); you are just stopping to borrow some resources.

> *"Where you are on your own ladder inside of your box determines which behaviors you can reach when visiting other libraries."*

Your Stress and Security come with the change in your environment. Your Unhealthy to Healthy behaviors are your response to that change. Without grasping that these are two separate continuums, you will be completely unaware of the Healthy Stress and Unhealthy Security blind spots of your Core Type and might stay stuck in your box.

Countertypes

The last blind spot I want to bring to your attention is the concept of "countertypes." Countertypes are a Subtype of each number that tend to behave in the exact opposite way that their core motivations and mindsets predict. In some ways, they are like "anti-stereotypes." If you are primarily a countertype, you are uncomfortable with your core motivations and average tendencies. You will tend to avoid your "Home" position on the map in favor of hanging out at other libraries, namely your Stress or Security Numbers, but possibly also your wings or the types that resemble your styles (leadership, learning, attachment, and so on), or even your culture or your traditions. Sometimes, being yourself isn't in your comfort zone, so you counter it.

I am primarily a Countertype 7. Most of the time, I prefer my Type 1 and Type 5 behaviors to be withdrawn, observe, have structure, or follow the rules, and will habitually default to them. Part of my growth journey is recognizing that the Fun Type 7 role, which I am able to play so naturally and intuitively, is a higher priority to closing the gap between my real self and my false self. This is how I earned the nickname "Lady Loophole" in some circles: I learned to research ways to "break the rules" without actually breaking the rules as a way to balance my instincts.

Depending on your Core Type, countertypes are typically explained by one of your Instinctual Variant Subtypes: Self-Preservation, Sexual (Social Mate), and Social (Social Order). The following are the countertypes for each type:

Type 8 - Social (Social Order)

Type 9 - Social (Social Order)

Type 1 - Sexual (Social Mate)

Type 2 - Self-Preservation

Type 3 - Self-Preservation

Type 4 - Self-Preservation

Type 5 - Sexual (Social Mate)

Type 6 - Sexual (Social Mate)

Type 7 - Social (Social Order)

You have all three instinctual variants of your type, but one will be your "Goldilocks" strategy that feels "just right" and is the most comfortable to you. This will be dynamic depending on your season in life and your experiences, preferences, or by the needs you are trying to meet: Survival, Social, or Self needs.

The Countertype 7 has the instinct for Social, meaning this is my go-to survival instinct.

If you are operating under the Social instinct, it does not mean you are a socialite. Sometimes it might mean the opposite. Social instinct simply means that you are paying attention to the *social order* or hierarchy of a group. You're trying to determine what societal role you should play that will increase your chances of survival. It actually addresses more of a Self-esteem need than a Social need. You're asking, "What role do I play in the group?" This is the primary instinct for Countertypes 7, 8, and 9. Instead of being self-indulgent, the Countertype 7 might sacrifice her own contentment and be focused more on creating shared experiences for the greater contentment of the group. Instead of being strong-willed and fighting for autonomy, Countertype 8 might stand in solidarity with the group and be supportive. Instead of sitting back and waiting for others to nudge him, Countertype 9 might take more initiative to participate in the decision-making for the group.

The Countertypes 1, 5, and 6 have the primary instinct of Sexual or Social Mate. Primitively, this is based on attracting a mate to procreate and maintain the species' survival. Practically, this doesn't necessarily mean a sexual partner but also seeking out friendships, business partners, or enemies. Sexual Types are less focused on intercourse and more on social rapport or chemistry with individual people. They are focused on belonging, relationship and other one-to-one *Social needs*. You're asking, "Whom do I connect with here?" This is true for all types with the Sexual instinctual variant, but for the countertypes the behaviors seem to go against their core motivations and mindsets. For example, instead of showing restraint, Countertype 1 might challenge the integrity of others with more zeal and fewer morals. Instead of being detached and private, the Countertype 5 might be a more transparent companion or be more confident in social situations. Instead of wavering, the Countertype 6 is more assertive and intimidating, testing to see whom she can trust.

The Countertypes 2, 3, and 4 have the primary instinct of Self-Preservation, which focuses on Survival needs, the bottom two levels of Maslow's pyramid. It's not just food, air, water, and shelter. This also includes employment, health, clothing, sex, finances, property, and so on. You're asking, "Am I safe and comfortable?" For the Countertype 2, instead of taking care of others, he might feel more entitled and manipulate others to take care of him. Instead of competing, the Countertype 3 might be more focused on accomplishing whatever it takes to put food on the table and pay the bills to have a secure future. Instead of focusing on suffering or melodrama, the Countertype 4 might be more self-sufficient to meet his own needs without complaint, almost masochistic in their determination to be lighthearted.

Even if you are not currently a countertype, you still have access to the tendency to survive by denying your core motivations and mindsets. Not being aware of that can be a huge blind spot. This is the blind spot that I credit for mistyping myself on four different Enneagram tests. I'm not giving you the full breadth of the Instinctual Variant Subtypes and Countertypes here in this book in case you are still in Typing Mode — for the sake of not distracting you from the top-down process of elimination. Once you are confident in your Enneagram Type and recognize your motivations and stress patterns, Subtypes become more practical for your personal growth and a great place to work with a coach or an accountability group.

So now you are aware of some of the blind spots of your Enneagram Type. If you're feeling a little overwhelmed, that's natural. Most people want to tackle their blind spots and show 'em who's boss. But often, that has the opposite effect. Like pushing a football under the water at the pool, it's going to blast out into the air at rocket speed as soon as you let it go.

When you are on your ladder in the average or unhealthy space, the rungs between you and where you want to be can also be a blind spot (depending on your Stance Reflex). If you are fast-paced or compliant-paced, you might try to reach higher shelves at your Security Number's library by skipping rungs... and then fall off the ladder. You can climb faster, but skipping rungs is risky. Awareness of the intermediate steps can help you move forward and create boundaries to keep yourself from falling off the ladder.

This is good news, though. It means it is ok to pace yourself. It's not about strong-arming your personality but balancing it so you can be stable. In the next part of the book, you'll learn a simple framework to help you achieve and maintain this balance and create healthy boundaries that keep you resilient to external circumstances. That's your *Personality Wellness* game plan!

PART IV

12

USING C.O.R.E. TO
IDENTIFY YOUR NEEDS

Being a cheerleader, I was friends with many of the football
players at Furman University. Greg was a 6'3", 300-pound
offensive lineman and practically my best-friend-slash-
bodyguard. When I started to write this chapter about creating
a *game plan*, I contacted him to get his football expertise and
inside information about having a playbook. I remember
listening to him complaining about practices back in the day,
but he never complained about head coach Bobby Johnson.

Coach Johnson had an outstanding 60-36 winning record as
Furman's head coach, taking the team all the way to the I-AA
National Championship Game. (After I graduated, of course. I

would have loved to cheer at that game!) After that year, Vanderbilt hired him to rebuild their program, which has always been at the bottom of the Southeastern Conference (SEC) rankings. His negative 15-43 loss record seemed to be disappointing after building such a winning reputation. Johnson said, "We had a lot of confidence in how we ran our program at Furman. We thought if we used the same principles, same work ethic, and the same things that we demanded from our players that we were going to have a chance to compete." Then he continues to say, "It doesn't guarantee anything."

If you are happy with your current game plan for your *Personality Wellness* because you are "winning" at balancing your life, what happens when circumstances change? A career change, a baby, a diagnosis, a divorce, an unexpected loss. It also doesn't guarantee anything. Using the same game plan may or may not work. To hold on to a position takes adjusting your balance. It looks so easy to spectators when you see cheerleaders get tossed in the air and caught with one arm or land on one leg. But it takes a lot of practice and a lot of core strength to maintain that balance.

Despite the drastic record upset, Bobby Johnson is still a highly respected coach and received the SEC Coach of the Year in 2008. I didn't have a relationship with Coach other than bidding "Congratulations" after a game or suddenly becoming mute with a starstruck goofy grin if I happened to see him in the training room. So I can't vouch for his personality personally. But my friend, Greg, has nothing but respect for the man, saying, "Coach Johnson epitomized professionalism, character, and work ethic," and has impacted him personally in how he now coaches and leads. Greg is currently a football coach and special education teacher in Dalton, GA.

"It isn't what you DO that makes a lasting, meaningful impression.
It's who you ARE that truly impacts people and the world."

Greg also shared that he believed Coach Johnson was so successful because he completely understood the type of student-athlete he needed to recruit. The prospects had to be good at football, but they also had to be good students and have a good attitude in order to be on the team. He was looking for the whole package and not necessarily the best players with the best stats. Even though the "football" goal was to build a great football team, the "bigger picture" goal was to build excellent people.

Performance matters, but character matters more. Johnson was famous for his "no cussing" rule on the field, not to be overbearingly proper, but to establish discipline, class, and respect among teammates. He said, "That was a means of trying to make our team mentally tougher and concentrate on the important things and not the peripheral things." Not only did he enforce this rule, but he modeled it too. In his four years at Vandy, twenty of his student-athletes earned All-SEC recognition. The school was also at the top for Academic Honor Roll recognition, including linebacker Hunter Hillenmeyer, who earned the prestigious National Scholar-Athlete Award in 2002. Johnson's focus on excellence in his players was a necessary building block needed to build a great football team.

When YOU are balanced, everything you DO will fall into balance. Even when current circumstances don't seem to favor you, you can have the resilience and core strength to hold firm and be excellent.

I walked away from my conversation with Greg with more than a simple playbook analogy to offer you. His admiration for Bobby Johnson showed me that those *"Being Me"* truths I shared in the Introduction of this book really are universal truths. Coach's story taught me:

1. You need to know what you're looking for in the bigger picture.

2. You need boundaries that establish discipline, class, and respect.

3. You need resilience to be mentally tough to stay balanced and excellent.

Now that you understand how your personality is structured and how the Enneagram can help guide you to overcome your blind spots, you might be asking yourself:

"Now what? Where do I start?"

Like any exercise trainer will attest, you need to strengthen your core. Not only to improve your balance but also to prevent injuries. That's the idea behind the *C.O.R.E. framework* you'll learn in this last part of the book. It's a game plan structure that you can use to create the plays in your *Personality Wellness* playbook. With practice, you'll build up your personality's core to improve your balance through self-regulation while also building resilience to "prevent injuries" when circumstances change. In other words, you can regain control of yourself on the inside when chaos is around you on the outside.

But first, I want to bring to your attention two illusions your brain creates that might trick you and get in the way of your game plan.

The Truth Illusion

A few years ago, a post blew up on the internet and spurred the great Yanny vs. Laurel debate. While listening to an audio clip, participants were asked if they heard the name "Yanny" or "Laurel," and some of the comments got heated about who was right. The people on Team Yanny thought the people on Team Laurel needed a hearing check and vice versa. And then there were some people that could hear both names at different times!

Which is the Truth?

The truth is that everyone has their own truth based on how their body senses the incoming information. When Britt Yazel, a neuroscience doctoral student at the University of California, Davis, filtered out all the sound above the frequency 4.5 kilohertz, he illustrated how it "takes away the entire perception of hearing the word 'Yanny' and all you get is the word 'Laurel.'" Yazel says, "If you lose the high frequencies, the illusion goes away." Likewise, if the lower frequencies are filtered out, all you will hear is "Yanny."

Because some people have different frequency sensitivities, people will hear different words. But Yazel also explains that "the brains themselves can be wired very differently to interpret speech." For example, if you encounter similar words to "Laurel" in your everyday life, you're more likely to hear "Laurel." But if you work as a nanny, or your best friend's name is Manny or Danny, or if you call your granny every day, You might hear "Yanny" more clearly.

This is how your personality's nature and nurture also influence your perceptions of the world. You are already primed to hear a subset of the whole truth and then interpret it in a meaningful or logical way based on your experiences. And sometimes, it is hard to un-hear once those experiences have been ingrained. If you've ever misheard song lyrics, as in the 80s hit "Blinded by the Light," you know what I'm talking about.

Your Enneagram Type has core motivations that serve as filters ingrained into your psyche and have been reinforced your entire life by your perceptions. Of the 11 million bits of information your body senses per second from your environment, you must fill in the gaps of the 99.9996% that your conscious awareness didn't register. According to Nina Kraus, a Northwestern professor of neurobiology who runs a laboratory on how humans process sound, people will fill in the gaps of their hearing when faced with a noisy context. In one exercise, she plays a poor quality, staticky audio clip of a voice saying something completely inaudible. She then followed that with a high-quality version of the same clip revealing what was said. When Kraus then replayed the initial inaudible clip a second time, participants could easily make out the correct sounds. She concludes that much of what you hear is about what you're expecting to hear. That expectation is what shapes your reality or your truth.

When your truth seems consistent with other people's truths, you get validated; there is no friction and no pause. When it doesn't seem consistent or gives you a "noisy context," you start comparing. And if you can't reconcile the differing views, it might become a "threat" to your way of perceiving the world. When your truth is threatened, your survival is threatened.

Then your *Personality Reflex* is activated and must go to completion.

Our brains trick us when we assume that my truth and your truth are the same, and we become alerted. But as you have seen with the nine stereotypes of the Enneagram, all nine operate under their own primary truths. Each has different motivations, strengths, and mindsets shaping their core values and perspectives. And by default, the intention behind your average behaviors and how those behaviors are experienced are very different. You are each hardwired to protect your own truth as a manner of survival. Even when you're focused on someone else's truth, your truth always wins, either consciously or unconsciously.

"As soon as you recognize that there are other valid truths or perspectives, your brain and body start becoming more open and more creative to the solutions that help your triggered situation — instead of leaving you with helpless, unlovable, or worth less feelings that lead to self-sabotage."

More recently, the "Bart Simpson Bouncing" auditory illusion has gone viral on the internet. But this time, you're given nine different phrases to read while listening to a crowd chanting to the tune of "La Donna è Mobile." What you hear seems to change to whichever phrase you are reading. If you can hear at least two different phrases (I can make out all nine of them!), that opens up the humbling possibility that your perception might not be the capital T Truth. Diana Deutsch is a Professor of Psychology at the University of California, San Diego, and explains that these "illusions show that the auditory system does not faithfully transmit the sound information as it arrives at our ears, but alters and reorganizes this information in various ways."

As soon as you recognize that there are other valid truths or perspectives, your brain and body start becoming more open and more creative to the solutions that help your triggered situation — instead of leaving you with helpless, unlovable, or worth less feelings that lead to self-sabotage. With renewed perspective comes more compassion and empathy for others and yourself. You begin to develop self-regulation skills, balancing your *Personality Tripod*, so you feel more stable and secure.

The Fear Illusion

The skill of self-regulation first starts with accepting that negative triggers are fear-based, and second, the discernment between self-protecting fear and self-sabotaging fear. In other words, you're asking, is it genuine survival fear, or is it a false fear?

Have you ever heard that fear is an acronym F.E.A.R. which stands for False Evidence Appearing Real? Running away from a hungry lion chasing you is genuine survival fear. But, that's not what this acronym is referring to. It means that sometimes we perceive threats that aren't real. Sometimes we make assumptions: "Why hasn't Beth returned my texts? Oh no, she must be mad at me" When in reality, Beth was on a camping trip and didn't have a signal. False fear turns into self-sabotage when you lack the skills to see that there is no real threat. But when you can discern that there is no proverbial lion chasing you, you can quickly self-regulate and dissipate the impact of your false fears.

My brother used to tell me really morbid things. He is five years older than I am, and like any good big brother, he loved to mess with me. He used to tell me that when a dog lies down on its side, if its front legs were bent, he was sleeping, but if its legs were straight, he was dead. It's ridiculous, I know, and obviously, this is not true, but I believed him and would have panic attacks whenever I saw my dog outside sleeping with her legs stretched out.

How was I able to overcome this false fear? At first, my reaction was to freak out, scream for my brother that the dog was dead, and then he would go outside and pretend to bring the dog back to life by gently bending one of her legs. If my brother wasn't around, I would hide my view of the dog until he got home to remedy the situation. One day, I finally got brave and approached the dog, confident that I could just do it myself. As I got closer, I slowed down and just stared at her while I gathered up my nerves to touch my dead dog. That's when I saw her breathing and realized the truth: the REAL truth — Truth with a capital T. It wasn't a perspective issue anymore. The "straight legs equal dead dog" was no longer a rule in my reality. I changed my (little t) truth, which is now consistent and aligned with the capital T Truth.

Capital T Truth is always balanced or neutral, always brings about peace or happiness, is always good or right, and never changes. But when there's a misalignment between your (little t) truth and the capital T Truth, you are vulnerable to fear. Whatever you've been told or what you've perceived appears very real to you. Your brain has been primed to cut through the "noisy context" and apply the rules of your reality.

The nine types of the Enneagram explain nine core fears:

- The fear of being controlled and losing your autonomy
- The fear of being disconnected, left in chaos
- The fear of being corrupted or being negatively influenced
- The fear of being needy or a burden on others
- The fear of being a fake, a failure, or inauthentic
- The fear of being a copy, unoriginal, or not special
- The fear of being depleted, left without resources
- The fear of being unprepared, unsupported, or blindsided by the unknown
- The fear of being deprived or having no options

Maybe you can relate to each of these fears on some level, but you are primarily vulnerable to one fear that can surface whenever there is a misalignment between your truth and The Truth. The *C.O.R.E. framework* allows you to get closer and face your fears, like when I braved going outside to revive my dog on my own. The more you look at it, the better you can see the REAL truth. You can rewrite the rules of your reality and get into alignment with The Truth, your core and original design. It is a decision to seek a perspective higher than your conscious awareness and climb the ladder out of your box.

> *"If you want to get your needs met successfully, you need to be aware of these illusions of the truth and fear, as you create your game plan."*

Identifying Your C.O.R.E. Needs

If Coach Johnson sent his players onto the field without a game plan, there would be inevitable chaos! In Greg's words, "The chaos might work for a short time, but a team would self-destruct if there were not a good plan in place."

So what does it take to create a good game plan? If you Google game plan definition, you'll get back "a strategy worked out in advance." But there's so much more to it. A game plan is a framework worked out in advance that strategically walks you through the process of overcoming obstacles, so you keep moving forward. Let's break that down. This is what makes a good game plan:

- It is a framework — Frameworks are foundations. It isn't the details of the plays but the structure to create the plays in the playbook. This allows you to change the play without needing to change the goal. It also gives you something to refer back to if you've gotten disrupted or become distracted, especially when following the dopamine.

- It's worked out in advance — Preparation increases the probability of success. Greg explained to me coaches pour hours into preparing for a game, watching films of the opposing team to look for patterns, going over stats, collaborating with fellow coaches who have faced this same opponent before, until they "know what the other coach was thinking better than he did." This book has prepared you for this moment, showing you the patterns of your personality, motivations, strengths, mindsets, and blind spots.

- It assumes there will be obstacles — There's always a villain in a story that gets in the way of your goals. How boring would the Harry Potter series be, though, if there was no Severus Snape to ponder over his villainhood? When you assume obstacles, you won't be completely blindsided by them. Yes, you can be annoyed by them. You're only human, after all, looking for the path of least resistance. However, this assumption will allow you to create more effective boundaries to be resilient.

- It's strategic — Strategy assumes the bigger picture of your goal. The offensive goal in football isn't always to get you into the end zone after every single play but to keep moving the line of scrimmage closer to the goal line. And sometimes you have to fall back to advance. Where most personal growth journeys fail or stagnate are in the setbacks. Go back to the game plan, and use those setbacks as a setup for a comeback!

- It's a process — Processes give you the steps. When you have clear next steps, it is easy to take action. And action really is what makes a plan a plan. A plan without action is only a pipe dream. Don't just create the game plan, but also go out onto the field and play the game.

Creating a game plan of getting to your C.O.R.E., or in alignment with The Truth, is simply a game plan for how to fulfill your life's purpose (*Oh, is that all?*).

Simple does not mean easy. But purpose is the universal motivator. Meaning gives way to action. Goals set the stage for strategy. And vision provides the bigger picture that allows you to focus. The *C.O.R.E. framework* helps you stay on track with your life's purpose game plan with four easy-to-remember steps to help you identify your needs and get back to your C.O.R.E.: it is an acronym for *Check*, *Own*, *Renew*, and *Engage*.

More specifically, for this book:

- Check Yourself
- Own Your Feelings
- Renew Your Mind
- Engage Your Power

Notice each step is a progression of integrating your body, heart, mind, and soul. This is the holistic approach to balancing your *Personality Tripod* by examining your Core Strengths, Core Motivations, and Core Values to reach your Core Power for your purpose.

The overarching theme of the *C.O.R.E. framework* is "*Being You,*" not anyone else. When you stay in your own lane and stop checking up on others to compare progress, you can better own your feelings and stop playing the blame game. This also allows you to focus on being of your own mind, not conforming to others, taking responsibility for your unique gift or superpower that only you are perfectly equipped and designed to give to the world.

But what if you don't know your life's purpose? Or maybe you already know your purpose and have a vision but struggle daily with procrastination, through avoidance or ineffectual busywork. Perhaps you cannot hold that focus or passion due to your circumstances. Or you are so frustrated at the lack of progress you are making, even though you know you are doing everything "by the book." You need a framework you can implement RIGHT NOW.

In the next chapter, I'm going to share the more profound concepts of the *C.O.R.E. framework* that I've developed over the years coaching clients, students, and my children to help them regulate themselves by understanding what they need and how to get in the proper frame of mind to meet those needs.

Use the handy *C.O.R.E. framework* worksheet to guide you through the rest of this book. It will help you reflect on your own personality as you read and develop your game plan. You can download it for free by going to

https://go.unboxenneagram.com/beingyoubook.

Scan code to download the free
C.O.R.E. framework worksheet

You don't need to know your Enneagram Type to use this framework, but knowing it does tend to expedite the process of self-regulation and balancing the legs of your *Personality Tripod* so you feel stable. However, since mistyping is so common, you must be confident you are working with your proper Core Type if you want to see the growth results you are expecting for a particular type. Even so, you will be equipped with practical starting points for each type, and you'll have a handy mnemonic in your long-term memory to refer to during your journey of what you've learned in this book.

13

Using C.O.R.E. for Self-Regulation

One of my favorite props to use in my classes and coaching is a pendulum. It is a simple way to demonstrate the Human Nature of duality. You're swinging between two choices, two outcomes, two motivations, usually your desires and your fears. If you want to be confident, you want to guard against the fears of low self-esteem. But you also have to protect against the overconfidence of pursuing your desires, lest you become arrogant, which is also associated with low self-esteem. Swinging too hard to one end will turn the pendulum into a wrecking ball, undermining your efforts to overcome your fears and meet your needs. Self-regulation is being able to stop or minimize the swing of your pendulum.

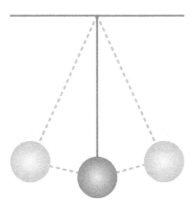

To Be You, or get to your core, you must take control and be the authority of your life's purpose. Just like a dam regulates the flow of water, or your thermostat regulates the temperature in your house, you must have a goal and learn to make adjustments to maintain your alignment to that goal. If you have your thermostat set to 72 degrees F, it will monitor the current temperature and assess if any changes need to be made. If the environment goes one degree above 72, your air conditioner will kick in. Once the current temperature returns to 72, your air conditioner will turn back off. Those are two plays in the thermostat's game plan!

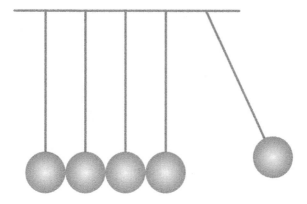

Your game plan can start that simply. As you become more aware, you'll develop habits and systems that work together to integrate your life toward your ultimate purpose or calling. Once developed, this self-regulation will be seamless, and your pendulum will be more like Newton's cradle. Even though the outside balls are battering the inside balls, those inside balls are stable and barely affected.

I have used the *C.O.R.E. framework* in several contexts to help clients of different personalities with their businesses, family systems, relationships, self-care needs, or discovering their life's purpose. Katherine realized she had spent almost twenty years successfully running a company as General Manager and found she hated her job. Using an earlier variation of this framework, she decided to quit, go back to school and become a nurse. She completed her education and chose to become an oncology nurse. Years later, when her husband fell ill with cancer, she was able to take care of him and had more confidence in providing and asking for what he needed. Talk about convenience! She was so grateful that she stayed true to herself, despite the many obstacles she faced that required different plays — some worked and some didn't. She was pushing 50 and going back to school with more spry 20-somethings, it was a huge income adjustment for her, and she was humbly reminded daily that she wasn't the boss anymore. Nevertheless, her game plan was always for becoming a nurse, and she never gave up.

This framework flexibility allows you to create different plays for your playbook for various situations to adjust your overall life's game plan. You'll have lots of plays, but you only need to include the plays that will get you closer to your purpose.

> *"This framework flexibility allows you to create different plays for your playbook for various situations to adjust your overall life's game plan."*

The *C.O.R.E. framework* walks you through the process of examining the three legs of your *Personality Tripod* at different levels of your consciousness. Once you're able to recognize blind spots and define your values, you'll know how to keep your tripod balanced and stable. Not only is it validating, but it is also motivating!

Use the *C.O.R.E. framework* worksheet that you can download for free at https://go.unboxenneagram.com/beingyoubook to guide you through this chapter. In this book, I want to cover the concepts of each step by focusing on the most primitive use of the framework for getting to know your *Personality Reflexes* as a body system. That way, you have the foundational basis for applying it to any situation you are facing that pulls you out of alignment.

"How do I know I'm out of alignment, Jen?"

C is for Check

Let me ask you this, "How do you know when your car needs an alignment?" The most obvious for me is that the steering wheel seems to have a mind of its own. I'm on a straight road, but the car pulls to the left. And when I slow down, the wheel might start to jiggle and feel a little unstable. But there isn't a "check alignment" light on the car's dash, just a "check engine" light. When that light turns on, you're alerted that something isn't correctly functioning under the hood. When you take your car in for repairs, don't they always offer to check the alignment? This isn't to squeeze another Ben Franklin out of you, but because tire alignment is often the root of many wear and tear issues that can lead to more costly problems down the road.

Your body also gives you signals that your spine is out of alignment. But did you know that back or nerve pain is usually the last indicator that something is off? For me, I waited until I was in tears before my first chiropractic visit. Because my spine was so out of whack, it took several visits before I could sit or stand without pain. However, pain is also the first symptom that goes away once you start treating the issue. Lack of physical pain does not necessarily mean your spine is aligned properly and perfectly functioning. You have a lot of organs in your body that don't have pain receptors that can still be adversely affected without your conscious awareness. Therefore, pain is not a very timely "check engine" light. Your misalignment has already upset other internal organs and processes before you ever register the pain.

Alignment means in the same path that allows free flow, with no barriers or obstacles blocking proper movements or actions, creating a path that leads to the same place or same goal. Everything works according to its designed purpose, efficiently, and with the most optimal results when things are in alignment. When you know that your spine is aligned, you can rest in the blessed assurance that your body can function properly.

If you notice, everything in nature follows a plan or a design or a cycle. There is the water cycle and the life cycle of plants and animals. Wild salmon instinctively know to leave their freshwater home to go to the saltwater sea. They know to eat a particular fatty diet so they have the energy to swim back upstream to their original home. There, they lay their eggs and start the cycle over again. When fishermen catch the adult salmon on their return trip to spawn, the fish are at their healthiest, ready to face the upstream battle. They are also at their pinkest with the most nutritionally dense meat for humans to eat. When the fish are raised in the salmon farms, their kibble diet strips them of their pinkness and their meat isn't as healthy for human consumption. The result is sub-par salmon. Farm-raised salmon who have escaped into the wild are sluggish and not equipped to survive predators. They also have low reproduction rates due to not having enough energy to swim up the river or not having a "home" river to return.

You are also in the animal kingdom, so your body has that same kind of intelligence or instinct. Your body knows and wants to return to normal functioning or "home"-eostasis. The salmon don't trap themselves on the farm, but we humans can hold ourselves captive, which compromises our own survival ability. You can sometimes actually RESIST being in alignment to the capital T Truth when change is more painful than the pain of staying the same, as with my recovery to fix my posture after months of compensating for my broken leg. The realization is in accepting that the pain is temporary but necessary to journey back to your personality's original design. Part of my game plan for my posture is getting regular adjustments for maintenance before pain rears its ugly head.

It would be best if you acknowledged your Survival Needs first. When you focus too much on your Social or Self-esteem Needs, your very foundation can crumble with nothing to show for your efforts. When your body is healthy, you have the healthiest relationships and play the most meaningful roles in your community. This is probably what is missing in the bigger picture of getting your needs met.

So the first step in the *C.O.R.E. framework* is C for Check. For self-regulation, you want to "Check Yourself" proactively and not reactively before the pain of conflict, disappointments, and other stresses rear their ugly heads. You cannot control stressors, but you can prepare for them by practicing self-care maintenance. Sometimes I forget to practice self-care as often as my body requires it. If you're busy like I am, it might not be practical to stop, drop, and meditate every time you notice something is "off."

Instead, consider micro-mindfulness. It's much easier to be mindful if you know what you are looking for. I started paying attention to a specific list of my body's signals. Before I would blow them off because I had become desensitized to them. These are some of the signals your body sends you as a clue that something is "off" and out of alignment. You can start here or build a custom list for the signals you already know you have.

- Shallow breathing

- Poor posture

- Tight muscles

- Clenched jaws

- Low energy levels

- Low libido

- Decreased appetite

- Cold hands or feet

- Swelling or bloating

- Joint, muscle, or nerve pain

- Allergies or illness

When you notice one of these on the list, try to identify one or two symptoms you can address at the moment. I start with breathing and posture because that's something easy to do while multi-tasking and pretty much goes hand in hand. I clasp my hands on top of my head and take a few intentional deep belly breaths. Sometimes, that will alert me to another symptom on the list.

In the beginning, you're just learning to recognize your body's signals. Don't pressure yourself to have an entire detailed plan of cutting out all the carbs in your diet before you're in good communication with your body. Eventually, you'll be able to start connecting the signals beyond your physiological Survival Needs to your safety Survival Needs that are affected by your core motivations, mindsets, and 9 Acknowledgment Languages™ of your Enneagram Type.

For example, I might ask myself, "Jen, are you content? What's got you anxious? Are you feeling trapped or deprived? Are you going too fast? Need a good ugly cry?" When I ask myself the right question, my body will respond accordingly. More often than not, when I acknowledge a blind spot or an issue that I'm resisting (like taking a break), my body feels a shift. Maybe I sit a little taller, or my muscles relax a bit, I might get a little boost of energy, or my intuition just kicks in and says, "Yep, you know what to do," and even though that choice might suck, I feel a little freer.

In chiropractic care, the goal is to return the spine to its original design. That way, your nerve signals can freely travel from your brain to the rest of your body without getting pinched or blocked. Likewise, when your little t truth is aligned with the capital T Truth of your core or original design, you will feel the freest, with no blocks in your clarity of purpose. As the saying goes, "The truth shall set you free."

Your ultimate Core Strength for survival is the beautiful way your body has been designed to function and heal itself for safety and comfort. Don't add to the stress by overworking it, taking on stressors that are not your burden to bear, or by judging yourself too harshly. This only perpetuates false stress and leads to burnout. This requires understanding the difference between real stress and perceived stress. Both activate your survival self-protection reflexes in your brain, but those reflexes are only helpful or healing when the stress is real.

"How do I know if the stress is real, Jen?"

O is for Own

Remember when going to the mall was the best way to one-stop-shop? You could get a greeting card, a new outfit, a quick lunch, and get your ears pierced while waiting for your glasses prescription to get filled. Terry and I even got our marriage license from the mall!

Each business at the mall has walls, a kiosk, a cart — an area they are responsible for to conduct their business. The Cheesecake Factory doesn't have the right to look at Abercrombie's accounting books or purchase their inventory. And when Coldwater Creek closed their doors, it wasn't Chick-fil-A's fault. All the businesses in a mall are independently responsible for their own success and failure.

Our lives are very much the same way. You have an independent truth and a unique combination of values, motivations, and strengths. That's your business. And the other little t truths or businesses in the mall of life? Not your business.

Unfortunately, there are no concrete walls, kiosks, or carts that house all of the different little t truths so that we can see physical boundaries. Out of sight, out of mind. How do you know you have crossed a boundary? In the food court, you can get the food you want and then intermingle and sit where you want. That can be dangerous, especially when you have a peanut allergy and someone eating Peanut Pad Thai sits next to you. You get up to move as quickly as you realize the risk (for survival), and the poor guy is sniffing his pits, wondering what he did to offend you, or muttering some choice words after you for being so rude. Real classy, huh?

Wouldn't it be nice if we could wear a sign that says "It's not you, it's me"? There would be no wondering, no misinterpretations, and no need for emotional overreactions. There would be a visual delineation of responsibilities, so you wouldn't need to put your body through stress over issues that are really non-issues.

Step #2 is O for Own. "Own Your Feelings" by thinking about which ones are yours to be responsible for in the first place. In the case of self-regulation, only focus on recognizing your own feelings because they matter and need protecting. Some personalities have an easier time getting in touch with their feelings than others. Still, unmet emotional needs are always at the root of your *Personality Reflexes,* no matter which Enneagram Type you are.

Labeling your emotions tells you precisely what you are responsible for and gives you context on establishing boundaries around them. These boundaries around your heart serve to protect your feelings or perspective and contain your emotional reactions tipped off by your Personality Reflexes.

If you struggle with labeling and containing your emotions, I've got good news!

Your Emotional Yardstick dialect will simplify the labeling for you. Depending on your Enneagram Type, you are experiencing a continuum of anger, shame, or fear. If you are a Type 2, 5, or 8, who are more aware and comfortable with your Emotional Yardstick, labeling is probably a piece of cake. Your boundaries will need to mostly be in place to contain your emotional reactions. But suppose you are one of the other six repressing or suppressing types. In that case, being able to correctly identify what you feel will allow you to start putting boundaries around them to feel safer.

As a Type 7, I thought I was just always angry when my needs weren't met. I didn't realize what I had actually been feeling but suppressing was fear and anxiety. I was putting boundaries up to protect and contain the wrong emotion, sabotaging my efforts to meet my needs.

Here is a summary of the Emotional Yardsticks for each type and their awareness and comfort level for expressing their dominant emotion. Remember that the continuum for anger can be anything from bothered to passion, shame: from pity to pride, and fear: from wary to confidence.

- **Type 8's** are aware and comfortable expressing emotions on the anger continuum.

- **Type 9's** are unaware and uncomfortable expressing emotions on the anger continuum, so they repress them.

- **Type 1's** are aware and uncomfortable expressing emotions on the anger continuum, so they suppress them.

- **Type 2's** are aware and comfortable expressing emotions on the shame continuum.

- **Type 3's** are unaware and uncomfortable expressing emotions on the shame continuum, so they repress them.

- **Type 4's** are aware and uncomfortable expressing emotions on the shame continuum, so they suppress them.

- **Type 5's** are aware and comfortable expressing emotions on the fear continuum.

- **Type 6's** are unaware and uncomfortable expressing emotions on the fear continuum, so they repress them.

- **Type 7's** are aware and uncomfortable expressing emotions on the fear continuum, so they suppress them.

You are responsible for responding to your reflex's triggers, but judgment leads to overreactions and vicious cycles that are hard to contain. Remember that your Emotional Yardstick functions to simply assign an emotional value to information to retrieve the memory more easily, or learn the lesson faster. This understanding can help you get to a neutral position, like the inside balls of Newton's cradle, when it comes to containing your emotional reactions. Own your feelings, without judgment, to neutralize them.

More importantly, you are not responsible for how other people respond to their reflex triggers. "It's them, not you." If someone else overreacts, it is none of your business. You can still care about someone else without taking responsibility for their feelings. That's what good humans do. It's called community, and thriving communities are interdependent. Thriving malls have many different businesses; they support each other by being each other's customers, offer word of mouth advertising, develop friendships among employees, and encourage each other during off-seasons and such.

> *"You can still care about someone else without taking responsibility for their feelings."*

Remember that your truth and their truth are not the same and that it is okay. In fact, you can say it is designed to be that way. How else could we all be so unique? You can be personable without taking things personally. Don't be fooled by the *Truth Illusion* by trying to close the gap between your little t truth and someone else's little t truth. Each of us only needs to close the gap between our own little t truth and the capital T Truth.

In the beginning, try to recognize the anger, shame, and fear in your behaviors. If you are already great at labeling your emotions, connect what you are feeling to the simple labels of anger, shame, or fear. Eventually, you'll be able to make more connections to your primary dialect of anger, shame, or fear and adjust your boundaries for each of the plays in your playbook to be more inline with your own Enneagram Type's core motivations. For example, if you are a Type 8 with that peanut allergy, you might ask yourself as you flee the food court irritated, "Am I angry because I feel controlled? Weak? Injustice to not be able to sit where I want to sit?" Being able to validate yourself without judging yourself gives you a more neutral perspective of what your personality as a body system is trying to accomplish. It's using stress in a helpful and healing way.

You wouldn't be feeling those emotions if something wasn't activated. Your brain is paying attention to the issue for a reason. It's communicating to you and giving your conscious awareness a clue that an unmet need is connected to this emotion below the surface of the lake waters. It's up to you to go fishing for it. Growth happens where effort is required. You might catch a lot of fish, but at the core of the net will be your Enneagram Type's core motivations.

Your ultimate Core Motivation for survival is getting your emotional or Social Needs met, specifically getting what you want and avoiding what you don't want. The feedback you infer from others will either validate or stand in the way of your needs. This can affect your self-esteem if you limit yourself to other people's responses. You'll tend to automatically invent meanings to justify behaviors, like the Pad Thai guy, which can lead to overreactions (or under-reactions) and create false stress (or false security) in your life. Boundaries help you stay disciplined and better connect with others.

Respecting your own boundaries to regulate your emotions allows you to think more clearly and compassionately, including self-compassion. Sometimes you can be blind to positive self-talk because you've settled into your box and closed the lid to get the sun out of your eyes. Even if you're on an average middle rung of your ladder, that isn't necessarily unhealthy; however, your box's lid is still closed to your potential, and you will talk yourself into staying where you are, believing it is positive self-talk.

"How do I open the lid to my potential, Jen?"

R is for Renew

How do you talk to yourself? Is it negative? Is it limiting? Do you say things like "I'm stupid," or "I'm not really good at cooking," or "I'm really bad for enabling him"? Or do you say,

"That's just how it is," or "I know how this is going to turn out," or "I don't know, and I don't care," or "If it ain't broke, don't fix it"?

This is dangerous because your self-talk becomes your truth. You have the power over your truth. It is what you believe it is.

And if you are standing on a middle rung with your lid closed chanting "It is what it is," then that is what it will always be.

Or maybe you have an alignment issue. Sometimes people set goals for themselves that aren't aligned with who they are. They get stuck, not understanding why their efforts are not producing any fruit. It's because they are planting the wrong seeds. Why would 5-foot me pursue a basketball career? I would get trampled, out-paced, and all of my shots would be blocked. That doesn't sound fun at all! That goal is not aligned with my personality (or my stature).

You can't change the circumstances of the past. You can't even change the events of the present. But you can change future scenarios with a simple mindset shift. Don't conform to the current circumstances of the world. Instead, it would be best if you believed that your future circumstances can change.

You are destined for the future you create in your mind. Are your thoughts about yourself focused on your strengths or your weaknesses? You might have taken an assessment in the past and were advised to focus on your strengths. That sounds like good advice, right? But just like dopamine, too much of a good thing can be just as destructive as having too little. You need a balance.

Your beliefs become your thoughts, Your thoughts become your words, Your words become your actions, Your actions become your habits, Your habits become your values, Your values become your destiny.
-Ghandi

Step #3 is R for Renew. To "Renew your Mind" is not simply changing your thoughts but reorienting them to an entirely new pattern of thinking. If a pendulum swings between your list of strengths and weaknesses, and your mindset only focuses on your strengths, you've set yourself up with a wrecking ball. Ignoring your weaknesses doesn't make them go away. It actually gives them more power to bring you down when they surface.

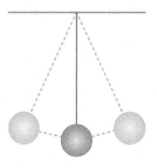

Your real strengths don't need as much focus because they come to you naturally. If you're already good at geometry and not so good at biology, you need to focus more on biology to graduate. But you don't want to ignore your geometry class completely either because you might lose the A you have in the course.

The good news is your personality strengths and weaknesses are not two separate subjects to tackle. They are actually in the same class. Your weaknesses are merely the unhealthy versions of your strengths. When the default mindset of your Enneagram Type is oriented to the duality of weaknesses vs. strengths, unhealthy extremes can compromise your core motivations and your bigger-picture purpose. Instead, look at them as a continuum that needs to be balanced.

Here is a summary of some of the stereotypes' mindsets, strengths, and weaknesses.

- **Type 8's** mindset to "overpower" can be a strength of willpower or weakness of oppression.

- **Type 9's** mindset of "inertia" can be a strength of togetherness or weakness of fusion.

- **Type 1's** mindset of "restraint" can be a strength of integrity or a weakness of resentment.

- **Type 2's** mindset of "flattery" can be a strength of nurture or a weakness of enabling.

- **Type 3's** mindset to "compete" can be a strength of self-assurance or a weakness of vanity.

- **Type 4's** mindset of "melancholy" can be a strength of endurance or weakness of self-affliction.

- **Type 5's** mindset to "detach" can be a strength of honesty or a weakness of insensitivity.

- **Type 6's** mindset of "doubt" can be a strength of dependability or weakness of duplicity.

- **Type 7's** mindset to "explore" can be a strength of immersion or weakness of escapism.

The irony is that the more aware you are of your weaknesses without this mindset shift, the more you might fear them. For example, if you are a Type 8, you might dial back your assertiveness out of fear of oppressing others and end up oppressing yourself. Or, as a Type 3, you might deny your competitive side out of fear of appearing vain and end up procrastinating or settle for second place out of a fear of success. Remember that F.E.A.R. stands for "false evidence appearing real." If it were a real stressor, your mindset reflexes would be helpful and healing, not self-sabotaging.

In the beginning, try to bust the *Fear Illusion* by monitoring your self-talk about your weaknesses. The power of the words "yet" or "used to" can take any self-talk that starts as negative or limiting, and transforms it into a hope for change in the future. Say, "I'm not really good at cooking yet" or "I used to enable him." Eventually, you'll start making the connection to your Enneagram Type's mindset and will notice whether it's being used as a dichotomy or as a continuum. If you are a Type 2, you might ask yourself a series of questions like, "Am I using flattery to encourage and enable his growth? Am I over-nurturing him and stunting his independence? Did he even ask for my help? Am I flattering myself that I'm capable of helping? Am I afraid he won't need me?"

The more related questions you ask, the more awareness you'll have to see your default mindset shift. Instead of seeing separate lists for weaknesses and strengths, you'll switch to measuring them as healthy or unhealthy according to your Enneagram Type's stress patterns. Once you've recognized you shouldn't shut down a "weakness" but simply redirect it up the ladder, you'll be able to pop open the lid of your box so you can scale your ladder more quickly. With no more lid blocking your vision, you'll have much more resilience or "bounce back-ability" when you find yourself on a lower rung.

Your ultimate Core Value for survival is building resilience to fend off the mind tricks that can negatively affect your Self-esteem needs. Self-care, boundaries, and resilience are the ultimate core needs for your *Personality Tripod* to balance upon. When the three legs are stable, then you can safely climb atop with peace of mind. This frees you to be more creative, think rationally, and spend more effort on tasks that make progress.

"How do I know when my tripod is stable enough, Jen?"

E is for Engage

Having a marathoner for a husband, I tried to get into running. Long-distance is still not my cuppa, but my first milestone goal after breaking my leg was to run a 5k. I remember when I trained for my very first 5k. I thought 3.1 miles was soooooo long. Why would I torture myself for at least half an hour, only to find that at the end, I'd feel nauseous, winded, and sore for days afterward? It didn't make sense to me, but in true Type 7 form, I decided to try it for the sake of trying it.

I mainly trained on treadmills during my lunch hour at the gym at work. Because I was so afraid of being bored, I felt I needed the TV to entertain me and distract me. I would glance between the metrics on the dashboard and *Days of our Lives* on the screen, watching the mileage meter increment up so slowly. Eventually, I didn't have to stop to walk once I got started. And then, one day, I looked down at the dashboard during a commercial, and I had passed 3.1 miles! But I didn't really want to stop. I was in a groove. Even though I was breathing hard, I felt like I could run forever.

This is called your flow state. It's a superhuman experience, a sweet spot where anxiety and boredom can't reach you. Psychologist Mihály Csíkszentmihályi describes it as a mental state of complete immersion in an activity. He tells Wired magazine, "The ego falls away. Time flies. Every action, movement, and thought follows inevitably from the previous one, like playing jazz. Your whole being is involved, and you're using your skills to the utmost."

In that I-could-run-forever moment, I understood how marathoners could do what they do. After that day, I didn't dread the treadmill anymore. I also didn't need the TV anymore. I started running on the track instead and would get lost in my thoughts. No longer distracted by daytime drama TV, I came up with some of the most creative solutions for my workplace culture project during my running time. I even started looking forward to it.

The Yerkes-Dodson Law describes the Eustress model I first introduced in Chapter 11 about your blind spots. Yerkes and Dodson also refer to the level of stress as your level of arousal or stimulation, meaning your stress plus your motivation. Overstimulation leads to your fight, flight, or fright response. Too much awareness when under pressure to perform creates a distressing situation of self-sabotage, where your survival reflexes lead to: your mind going blank, emotional dysregulation, and bodily dysfunctions.

The "calm" area under the curve is where boredom, depression, apathy, and false securities can impede your performance. If you are not challenged or believe a task has no purpose, you won't feel motivated to complete it. You'll do the bare minimum, which could be doing nothing.

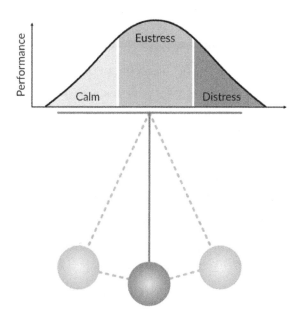

Your level of stress is also like a pendulum. Swinging to either extreme of the curve is not healthy. It's the balanced middle where you reach your optimal arousal state, flow, where "your whole being is involved, and you're using your skills to the utmost."

Step #4 is E for Engage. *Flow* is where you "Engage Your Power," when your whole being has been integrated with your core. Body, heart, mind, and soul come together for your peak performance to reach your Self-Actualization Needs or the very tippy-top of Maslow's pyramid (which he deems as the necessary step for transcendence or transfiguration). In other words, if you want true change to occur in your life, you must go through the steps of his hierarchy to unbox yourself, get to your core, and rise above your personality's ego needs.

C = Check Yourself, Practice Self-Care to meet your Survival Needs (Body)

O = Own Your Feelings, Establish Boundaries to meet your Social Needs (Heart)

R = Renew Your Mind, Develop Resilience to meet your Self-Esteem Needs (Mind)

E = Engage Your Power, Maintain a Healthy Balance to meet your Self-Actualization Needs (Soul or Core)

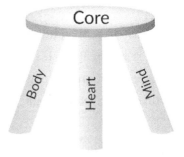

When your needs seem to be rejected, and you aren't communicating back to your inner self in a healthy way, you can block yourself from your Self-Actualization or flow. When you prioritize your *Personality Wellness*, you can reach your flow state quicker by ensuring your *Personality Tripod* is stable. This is when you are at your peak performance and your peak moral standards, creativity, spontaneity, and acceptance of and in alignment with capital T Truth. Stabilizing your Tripod and keeping it balanced is how you strengthen your core.

Your ultimate Core Purpose is *"Being You"*. Your Enneagram Type cannot determine this, but your Enneagram Type can be the guide on how to get there by showing you your blind spots. You *"Being You"* is the unique gift you offer the world, and only you are perfectly equipped and qualified to do the job. No one else can fill the role. Without it filled, the world is a little less whole.

I couldn't have asked for a more perfect conversation with my friend, Greg, to introduce the C.O.R.E. concept. It's a simple but powerful framework that I apply daily in my own life to stay on track and be aligned with my core. It's so meta that your purpose in life is finding your life's purpose as soon as you're born.

The three things I learned from our chat about Coach Bobby Johnson's story perfectly line up with your hierarchy of needs, the legs of your *Personality Tripod*, and the ego integration of your body, heart, and mind.

1. Know what you're looking for in the bigger picture --
   Safety and Comfort (Survival Needs)

2. Boundaries that establish discipline, class, and respect
   – Better Connection (Social Needs)

3. Resilience to be mentally tough to stay balanced and
   excellent (Self-Esteem and Self-Actualization Needs)

The microcosm and macrocosm of the plays in your playbook
that you use to create your life's game plan are as mind-blowing
as the day you realized that your hand isn't just a hand but is
made up of millions of atoms.

Atoms make up everything in the universe! Taking a closer
look, you'll see that an atom looks like its own tiny, microscopic
galaxy, with a nucleus (sun) and orbiting electrons (planets).
While atoms are busy following the laws of physics and
chemistry, are they aware that they are a part of a bigger picture
and serve a purpose of a higher function? The atoms in your

hand help you eat, wave hello, and write, type, or build — which, in part, meet your Survival, Social, and Self needs.

Likewise, you can view the Enneagram as your personality's microcosm or internal universe. But it serves a much bigger picture and a higher purpose. The Whole Enneagram also represents the macrocosm of the systemic relationships of your family and community. You're not just asking yourself, "Who am I?" but also, "Who am I in the world?"

Everyone is different, and everyone belongs. When you bring your whole self into the world, the world also becomes whole. How you interact with others creates a far-reaching ripple effect that transcends proximity and time.

In the next and final chapter, I'm addressing what you originally wanted to get out of the Enneagram in Chapter 1 to bring this full circle.

14

USING C.O.R.E. FOR GETTING ALONG WITH OTHERS

Finding Nemo is one of our family's favorite movies. It's about a clownfish who lost his wife and children in a barracuda attack, save for one little guy named Nemo. In the attack, Nemo was left with a "lucky fin" that was a fraction of the size it should be. The dad, Marlin, became hypervigilant about the dangers of the ocean, and understandably, sheltered Nemo in their sea anemone home that protects them. But Marlin essentially boxed Nemo in and allowed his fin to be a handicap that held him back instead of helping Nemo adjust.

Nemo starts school later than his peers, is encouraged to play on "sponge beds" where it's safer, and gets wrongfully accused of making the bad decision to swim into the open ocean. Being resentful of his dad's overprotection and disparaging comments about not being a good swimmer, Nemo willfully defies his dad to prove himself.

Because Nemo wasn't allowed to align with the core of his personality, he and his dad were not getting along. Marlin used his *Personality Paintbrush* and created an *Experience Gap* between them. Because of his own fear of the ocean, Marlin jumped to the conclusion that Nemo should be just as afraid, especially since he was "defective."

Within a family, there are systemic relationships. The parents and children have a relationship different from the husband and wife relationship, which is different from the sibling relationship. If you are also a teacher, there are systemic relationships at school, like teacher-to-student, teacher-to-parent, teacher-to-teacher, and teacher-to-principal. Likewise, in the community, there is a system of relationships directly or indirectly affected by you for every role you can play.

Whether you like it or not, the reality is that we are all connected, affected, and interdependent upon each other. You wouldn't be where you are right now without people, and you won't get to where you are going without people. So you need interpersonal skills to get along.

You've heard the phrases, "iron sharpens iron," and "misery loves company." People with the same personality traits or behaviors tend to flock to each other. When you have something in common, it's easier to understand each other and get along. However, health doesn't have to be a part of the picture of getting along. You can have two unhealthy people commiserating together and get along splendidly in their sarcastic banter or complaints, or maybe you form a codependent enmeshment that feels like you're getting along but is not very healthy. This will damage the system.

You can also have two healthy people, aligned to their core with self-care/boundaries/resilience, doing their purpose work, but still not have a healthy relationship with each other because they are too independent. Sorry, fellow introverts, we cannot escape the fact that we need people. Relationships exist, whether or not you are actively participating in them. You need to be just as aware of the impact of your absence as you are of your presence.

Both your presence and absences matter. If you don't show up to teach your class, adjustments must be made for your absence. Those adjustments directly affect the substitute teacher, the students, and the staff and can have a positive, negative, or neutral ripple effect into the world. Likewise, extroverts must balance this continuum so that you don't also turn its pendulum into a wrecking ball.

Not all roles are equal, but every person is important and deserves respect for the role they play. Mutualism aims to see the systemic relationship as symbiotic, like the clownfish and the sea anemone. Clownfish are immune to the toxic stings of the anemone's tentacles, so Marlin and Nemo stay safe from any future barracuda attacks. But the sea anemone also benefits. The fish's bright colors attract predators, which are then caught and eaten by the anemone. No one is taking advantage of anyone. It's a win/win relationship with mutual respect for each role.

In order to respect the relationship, there can be no demeaning, one-upping, envy, and (this is a hard one) impatience. When Marlin runs into Dory, a blue tang fish, she cheerfully offers to help him look for the boat that sped off with Nemo. If you're familiar with the movie, you know that Dory suffers from short-term memory loss and quickly forgets why she is with Marlin. He becomes angry at her for wasting his time and even says to her, "There's something wrong with you."

We've all had an encounter when someone didn't meet our expectations, or we let someone down because we fell short of their expectations. I can't boast that I've always responded in a healthy way, but the 9AL™ helped me recognize which part of my response was normal (neither healthy nor unhealthy). And the *C.O.R.E. framework* helped me realize which part I could improve to be healthier.

You can tweak the *C.O.R.E. framework* worksheet (download it for free at https://go.unboxenneagram.com/beingyoubook) to apply it to any scenario to help you bring creative solutions to your conscious-awareness!

"How can I use the C.O.R.E. framework to add a play to my game plan for getting along with others?"

Step 1: C is for Check

First, "Check Yourself" and make sure you are centered, aligned with your C.O.R.E., equipped with self-care, boundaries, and resilience. Ask yourself, "Am I ready to engage with this person? Am I being neutral or reactive? What am I fearing or avoiding? What is the bigger purpose for engaging? Will my core motivations be validated?"

When Marlin came at Nemo, and later Dory, with his accusations, he was following his stress patterns, full of anxiety, and not ready to engage. First, he was blind to the fact that his own fears were at the root of his doubt. It impeded his ability to make good decisions or face challenges, which made him reactive (his reflex). If you are not able to come to the relationship whole within yourself (the good, bad, and ugly), you might struggle to follow the next steps and be unable to get the results you're hoping for. If you deny your core motivations, you deny a part of yourself, no matter how selfish they might seem. This leads to wrecking balls of resentment, depression, or anxiety. So take extra time if you need to take a few deep breaths, grab a healthy snack, remind yourself of your boundaries and the healthy behavior options you can choose that align with your personality.

Step 2: O is for Own

Second, "Own Your Feelings" by checking for evidence of the *Truth Illusion.* Ask yourself, "What is the *Experience Gap* here? Is there too much paint on my *Personality Paintbrush* that's distorting my point of view?"

By acknowledging that you have a different little t truth than the other person, you can stop trying to reconcile your truths. I don't mean ignoring the other person's point of view, but accepting it as valid. Marlin cannot change the fact that Dory has short-term memory loss. That is her reality, and he must accept it if he wants her help. He didn't know it when he was dismissing her, but Dory had a superpower that Marlin needed from her — she could read. Being able to read the address on the diver's mask that fell off the boat was what put them on the right path of *Finding Nemo.* If he didn't have Dory, he would have had little hope of finding a tiny fish in a vast ocean. What hope are you missing out on because an *Experience Gap* duped you into thinking that someone else was capital W Wrong?

Step 3: R is for Renew

Third, "Renew your Mind" by stepping into their shoes. If you are wired to protect your core desires and fears, so is the other person. By taking on the perspective of what you know about their personality, you can help debunk their *Fear Illusion*. Ask yourself, "What are they afraid of? What might their best intentions be? What are their blind spots that might be making them reactive or unresponsive?"

You never know the whole story. You only know the part revealed to you, which is a very small percentage. If you're only conscious-aware of 10% of your own mind, how much less of the other person's real story are you actually getting right? But you don't need the whole story. Dory didn't need to know what happened at the movie's beginning to help Marlin on his quest. She didn't even need to know what happened five minutes before!

Dory's memory loss didn't impede who she was at her core. Despite her flaws and naivety, you adore her character because you feel for her. Marlin began to renew his mindset about getting along with Dory when he saw her motives were pure and innocent. When he sees Dory bouncing in the jellyfish field, he starts to chastise her (his reflex) for being careless around the stingers. But he changes the escape strategy and turns it into a game, which is more aligned with her personality. Note that this was made easier on him since he was on his Security Path; a clownfish is already resistant to stings! Because he was connected to his core survival instincts, he could be present to think about Dory instead of himself and actually stopped the *Fear Illusion* before Dory had a chance to be afraid.

Step 4: E is for Engage

Last, "Engage your Power" with the other person. Engaging means involving the other person with your power, not to force it onto them or withhold it from them. Ask yourself, "What gift can I give them that will be helpful or healing? Can we come to a compromise without compromising each other's core?"

You want to help balance each other's *Personality Tripod*s, not attack them! You have a power that can help them, and they have a power that can help you. This isn't selfish but is acknowledging the systemic relationship between you and the other person in the bigger picture. I know it isn't always unicorns and rainbows. You can make the best, most perfect effort, and it may not be reciprocated by the other person. It is best to disengage if you can't offer them a gift that will not compromise your own stability. Don't let it hold you back. Reinforce their Tripod and protect yours. You've done your part even if you don't get acknowledged by them for it.

When Marlin points his fin, blaming Dory for dropping the diver's mask into the deep dark ocean depths, she pauses and offers, "Hey, Mr. Grumpy Gills. When life gets you down, you know what you gotta do?" then begins to sing her famous chant "Just keep swimming." Marlin comes around (even if he is whining about the song getting stuck in his head), and they are back on their quest together. The other person might also come around that quickly, or you might never witness an outward expression of the positive impact you've had on them. Regardless, find a supporting role instead of a controlling role so you can Be Yourself and they can Be Themselves.

The *C.O.R.E. framework* used for relationships is best used when you know both your and their Enneagram Types, or you at least have a grasp on the 9 Acknowledgment Languages™ to support and communicate by speaking their dialects. This requires you to understand your own dialects first to know what has been lost in translation. This is the work most people ignore or fail to see its significance.

In this book, you have learned the *purpose* of your personality and how to be *intentional* to follow it, the first two of three universal truths about *Being You* that I wanted to share and that compelled me to write this book.

In Part I, you learned how your personality is a body system, so its real purpose is survival. By switching your focus away from the nurtured aspect of your personality shaped by your environment or relationships, and reorienting yourself to look inward at your basic survival instincts, you learned that your personality is simply a reflex that your body is wired to perform automatically.

In Part II, you learned that mistyping is common because it is hard to distinguish between which behaviors are naturally you and which have been nurtured into you. You gained some visual mnemonics that will stick with you way beyond this book when you start analyzing your behaviors to discern which ones you can change and which ones you shouldn't change.

In Part III, you learned how to view the 9 Acknowledgment Languages™ as the unconscious reflexes of your personality, getting a more comprehensive view of what it means to be your Enneagram Type based on the colors of your Triads.

In Part IV, you learned the simple yet versatile *C.O.R.E. framework* to help you self-regulate and navigate your role in the world.

The last universal truth, "*You have to be aware of your progress (or lack thereof),*" is up to you now.

You have the ground-laying concepts needed for unboxing the Enneagram to support your own growth and for effectively helping others. Implementing the concepts is the real work. I hope you find a community of like-minded learners who want to be their best, like the UBU Community. With the objective support and accountability for meeting your Survival, Social, and Self needs, you'll be better positioned to overcome your blind spots and get an accurate read on your progress.

Transformation in your life requires seeing the box you are already in so that you can rise above your personality's ego needs and realize your potential and unique gift in the world. But you cannot ignore those foundational needs that power up your wiring. When you are plugged into your core, you'll not struggle to find your purpose or calling to reach your happiness, fully satisfied with no regrets. Unboxing the Enneagram goes beyond the curiosity of Unboxing You — it unleashes the power of *Being You*.

Appendix

Glossary of Terms

9 Acknowledgment Languages (9AL) ™ - A UBU concept referring to the framework developed by Jen P. Higgins that gives structure to how your experiences get translated through the survival nature of your personality. Also used as 9 starter points for your personal development and building relationships.

Amygdala - The part of the brain that performs a primary role in the processing of memory, decision making, and emotional responses.

Association - A Rehearsal strategy for Learning. The process of connecting incoming information to information already stored in your memory.

Attention - The 2nd stage of Learning. The process of prioritizing the significance of incoming information received from your environment.

Attention Filter - One of the 9 Acknowledgment Languages™ describing how incoming information is internally processed and filtered according to your level of attention. Dialects are: Impact, Image, Security.

Blind Spots - Unconscious areas of your personality that drive your behavior.

The Box - A visual representation of your ego personality.

Centers Blind Spot - One of the 9 Acknowledgment Languages™, describing the domain of experience (Center of Intelligence) that is unconsciously overlooked. Dialects are: Action-blind, Emotional-blind, Thought-blind.

Centers of Intelligence - An Enneagram triad group, often referred to as the Centers, used to describe the three primary domains of experience: Moving Center, Feeling Center, Thinking Center.

Centers Reflex - A UBU concept referring to the automatic internal processing reflex, characterized by the first four 9 Acknowledgment Languages™, in response to incoming information from your environment that frame your experiences.

Cognitive Bias - The tendency for you to process and interpret incoming information to confirm your own perceptions or ideas.

Cognitive Overload - When your working memory receives more information than it can handle comfortably and compromises memory or learning. Overwhelm.

Conscious Mind - Level of your mind which involves all of the things you are currently aware of and thinking about.

Control Tactic - One of the 9 Acknowledgment Languages™, describing how incoming information is managed or controlled so needs can be met. Dialects are: Resisting, Impressing, Sorting.

C.O.R.E. Framework - A UBU concept referring to the 4-step holistic strategic game plan to integrate your personality in any situation.

Core Motivations - Strong unconscious desires and fears that push you toward what you want, or repel you from what you don't want.

Core Strengths - Hard-wired unconscious abilities which come naturally, or with very little effort.

Core Type - Your true Enneagram Type.

Core Values - Fundamental unconscious principles or strongly-held beliefs that bring you joy when experienced or pursued.

Countertype - A subtype of your Enneagram Type that tends to behave in the opposite way that your Core Motivations typically predict. An "anti-stereotype."

Dopamine - A neurotransmitter chemical created in the brain that acts as a messenger to nerve cells in response to stimuli that are rewarding or punishing.

Disintegration - The opposite of Integration. The act of breaking down into pieces, losing cohesion or strength.

Emotional Yardstick - One of the 9 Acknowledgment Languages™, describing how incoming information from experiences are measured and appraised for storage into memory. Dialects are: Anger, Shame, Fear.

Enneagram - A personality typology tool using the unconscious motivations of nine distinct types as the driver for patterns of behaviors.

Enneagram Type - A personality profile represented by a single number (1-9) that corresponds to a pattern of behaviors based on one of nine core motivations.

Eustress - A level of stress, sometimes referred to as "good stress", which neither overstimulates nor understimulates you and maximizes overall performance.

Executive Functions - A set of cognitive processes needed for the cognitive control of behavior. Performs the primary role of planning, selecting and monitoring behaviors to reach a goal. Control of attention, inhibition, working memory, cognitive flexibility, reasoning, and problem-solving.

Experience Gap - The difference between the intention of your behavior and the perception of that behavior, leading to frustration or misunderstanding.

Experience Gate - One of the 9 Acknowledgment Languages™, describing how incoming information from your environment is experienced or sensed. Dialects are: Body, Heart, Mind.

Fear Illusion - A UBU concept referring to when information from your environment is perceived as a threat when a threat does not exist.

Flow State - Mental state of complete immersion and energized focus, engagement, and enjoyment of an activity. "In the zone."

Game Plan - A strategic framework of steps planned out in advance to overcome obstacles and reach a goal.

Growing Mode - The second stage of your Enneagram journey when you are using your confirmed true Enneagram Type, or Core Type, for Integration to improve your *Personality Wellness*.

Growth Path - The dynamic path of an Enneagram Type when you intentionally choose healthy behaviors of your Core Type.

Hippocampus - The part of the brain that performs a primary role in the consolidation of information from short-term memory to long-term memory.

Homeostasis - The tendency toward a relatively stable equilibrium within a system or physiological processes.

Instinctual Variants - Also called Instincts. Subtypes of an Enneagram Type used to describe the continuum of behavioral responses according to primal survival instincts: Self-Preservation, Sexual, Social.

Integration - The act of bringing together smaller components into a single system that functions as one or as a whole. In this book, it refers to *Personality Wellness* and balancing the legs of your *Personality Tripod*.

Ladder of Awareness - A UBU concept referring to the Levels of Health of your Core Type.

Learning - The cognitive process of collecting, storing, and recalling information from memory. The 4 stages are Sensory, Attention, Rehearsal, and Retrieval.

Levels of Health - Also called Levels of Integration or Levels of Development (credit to Don Richard Riso). The nine levels on the continuum of behaviors from unhealthy to average to healthy. Represented by the *Ladder of Awareness* in this book.

Library of Behaviors - A UBU concept referring to an Enneagram Type's ability to adapt by adopting stereotypical behaviors of other Enneagram numbers.

Mistyping - When a person assigns themselves an Enneagram Type that is not their true Core Type.

Narrative Approach - An effective method to discover your Enneagram Type through dialogue with a certified Enneagram Coach who is trained to ask you the right non-leading questions, including the appropriate follow up questions.

Neuroplasticity - The ability of the brain to adapt and reorganize functionality as a result of experience.

Overlay - A mask or layer of personality formed through experiences (style, culture, trauma, routine, etc.) that may or may not obscure the Core Motivation of an Enneagram Type.

Pace Style - One of the 9 Acknowledgment Languages™, describing the speed of processing incoming information. Dialects are: Slow, Fast, Compliant.

Personality - A pattern of behaviors you employ as a strategy to get what you want or avoid what you don't want.

Personality Paintbrush - A UBU concept referring to the bias of experiencing the world according to your own personality.

Personality Reflex - A UBU concept referring to the unconscious internal and external automatic responses of your personality.

Personality Spectrum - A UBU concept referring to the wide range of unique personalities.

Personality Tripod - A UBU concept referring to the three traits of personality: Motivations, Strengths, Values. In this book, it refers to the three core traits governed by the unconscious mind: Core Motivations, Core Strengths, Core Values.

Personality Wellness - A UBU concept referring to the part of your health wellness for optimizing healthy behavioral responses to support the nature of your personality. The act of Integration.

Prefrontal Cortex - The part of the brain known as the "personality center" and the portion of the brain that fully develops last (late adolescence). Performs a primary role in reasoning, decision making, personality expression, and social cognition.

Primal Self-Protection Mode - The unconscious automatic response of your body, heart, and mind when there is a shift away from homeostasis.

Rehearsal - The 3rd stage of Learning. The process of storing information into memory, primarily by repetition and association.

Repetition - A Rehearsal strategy for Learning. The process of repeated exposure to information in an effort to store it into memory.

Retrieval - The 4th stage of Learning. The process of recalling information stored in memory. Remembering.

Retrieval Failure - The inability to recall information stored in memory. Forgetting.

Security Number - The Enneagram number associated with your Core Type whose behaviors you adopt when feeling secure.

.**Security Path** - The dynamic path represented by the line from your Core Type to your Security Number on the Enneagram diagram.

Self Needs - Refers to the fourth and fifth stages of Maslow's hierarchy of needs: Self-Esteem (developed through Self-Respect, independent of outside influence) and Self-Actualization.

Self-Preservation - Primal survival instinct for the need to be safe and comfortable. Associated with the Self-Preservation Instinctual Variant Subtype for your Core Type.

Self-Preservation Instinct - The Instinctual Variant Subtype of your Core Type that influences your behaviors, characterized by the need to protect and conserve yourself and your resources. Abbreviated as "sp."

Sensory - The 1st step of Learning. The process of collecting information from your environment through the senses: see, hear, smell, taste, touch, position, and balance.

Sexual Instinct - The Instinctual Variant Subtype of your Core Type that influences your behaviors, characterized by the need to connect with others and form one-to-one relationships. Abbreviated as "sx."

Spaced Repetition - A Rehearsal strategy for Learning. The process of repeating the exposure of information at longer intervals in an effort to store it into memory.

Social Instinct - The Instinctual Variant Subtype of your Core Type that influences your behaviors, characterized by the need to find a meaningful role within a system or group of people. Abbreviated as "so."

Social Mate - Primal survival instinct for the need to attract a mate and procreate. Associated with the Sexual Instinctual Variant Subtype of your Core Type.

Social Needs - Refers to the third and fourth stages of Maslow's hierarchy of needs: Love and Belonging, and Self-Esteem (developed through the Respect of others).

Social Order - Primal survival instinct for the need to play a role in a group or community according to a hierarchy. Associated with the Social Instinctual Variant Subtype for your Core Type.

Social Style - One of the 9 Acknowledgment Languages™, describing your position in respect to others to get your needs met. Dialects are: Avoiding, Confronting, Abiding.

Stances - An Enneagram triad group, loosely based on work of psychoanalyst Karen Horney (pronounced horn-eye), used to describe the posture, attitude, or standpoint you take in relationship to others for getting your needs met: Withdrawn Stance, Aggressive Stance, or Dependent Stance.

Stances Reflex - A UBU concept referring to the automatic external processing reflex, characterized by the last five 9 Acknowledgment Languages™, in response to controlling incoming information from your environment to meet your needs.

Stereotype - Greek word meaning "solid form". A way to generalize people or ideas to quickly convey expectations.

Stress Number - The Enneagram number associated with your Core Type whose behaviors you adopt when feeling stress.

Stress Path - The dynamic path represented by the line from your Core Type to your Stress Number on the Enneagram diagram.

Subconscious Mind - Level of your mind that holds memories and knowledge which you are not presently actively aware of but can retrieve and recall when needed.

Subtypes - Any variation of behaviors within your Core Type. The lower level of the Enneagram hierarchy used when typing. Common subtypes are Wings and Instincts.

Survival Needs - Refers to the first two stages of Maslow's hierarchy of needs: Physiological Needs and Safety/Security Needs.

Temperament - A term used by psychologists and pediatricians to describe a person's inborn traits and natural predisposition as it affects behaviors.

Thalamus - The part of the brain that performs a primary role of relaying sensory signals, including motor signals and the regulation of consciousness, sleep, and alertness.

Timeline Blind Spot - One of the 9 Acknowledgment Languages™, describing your orientation to time which is unconsciously overlooked. Dialects are: Present-blind, Past-blind, Future-blind.

Timeline Focus - One of the 9 Acknowledgment Languages™, describing your orientation to time used to give context to incoming information. Dialects are: Past-referencing, Future-referencing, Present-referencing.

Triad - A set of three Enneagram Types. The highest level of the Enneagram hierarchy used when typing. Common triad groups are Centers and Stances.

Truth Illusion - A UBU concept referring to the difference between an individual's perception (little t truth) and the actual truth (Capital T Truth).

Typing Mode - The first stage of your Enneagram journey when you are still in the process of identifying your Core Type, that is, your true Enneagram Type.

Unconscious Mind - Level of your mind that holds automatic functions and responses to stimuli that are not governed or directly accessed by the Conscious Mind.

Wings - Subtypes of an Enneagram Type used to describe the continuum of behaviors between the two numbers on either side of your Core Type on the Enneagram Diagram. Denotation example: 7w8 is read "seven wing eight" to describe Type 8 behaviors employed for a Type 7 motivations.

Sources

Beatrice Chestnut, PhD. 2013. *The Complete Enneagram*. She Writes Press. Berkeley, CA.

Lisa Cron. 2012. *Wired for Story*. Ten Speed Press, an imprint of the Crown Publishing Group, a division of Random House, Inc. New York, NY.

Karen Horney, MD. 1942. *Self-Analysis*. WW Norton & Company Inc. New York, NY.

Jonah Lehrer. 2009. *How We Decide*. Houghton Mifflin Harcourt Publishing Company. New York, NY.

Amir Levine. 2010. *Attached*. Penguin Group (USA) Inc. New York, NY.

Sandra Maitri. 2005. *The Enneagram of Passions and Virtues*. Penguin Group (USA) Inc. New York, NY.

Don Richard Riso and Russ Hudson. 1999. *The Wisdom of the Enneagram*. Bantam Books. New York, NY.

Don Richard Riso. 1990. *Understanding the Enneagram*. Houghton Mifflin Co. Boston, MA.

Mary K Rothbart, PhD. 2011. *Becoming Who We Are*. The Guilford Press. New York, NY.

Bessel van der Kolk, MD. 2014. *The Body Keeps the Score: Brain, Mind, and Body in the Healing of Trauma*. Penguin Random House LLC. New York, NY.

Acknowledgments

"I should write a book" has been a recurring thought of mine for as long as I can remember. I even wrote a children's book back in 2007, but I only took it semi-seriously and it never got published. It's still on my PALM pilot somewhere in the basement. On New Year's Eve of 2020 in the final minutes before ringing in 2021, with dreamy eyes and full of hope, I added, "Write a Book" on my vision board, right next to my podcast goal, and family cruise vacation. This time, I actually did it! But not without the prodding, cheering, and prayers from my family, friends, and launch team.

I would not have been able to write this book without my family, especially because they provided most of the stories: my man-crush, Terry, and sons, Eric and Ryan, in whom I am well pleased; my parents, Bernie and Elba, who humbly take relationship coaching from me, their youngest offspring, even though they have been married for over 55 years; my bestest siblings, Melanie and David, and my "BCF," Carina. You all are the inspiration behind why I am motivated to understand my own personality, blind spots, and to stay connected to my core. It's how I try to be the best wife, mom, daughter, sister/cousin for you. Thank you, fam.

Special thanks go to Terry, my hubby of 25 years (so far). I'm so grateful for the armor of steel you put on these last few months when I was hangry or up past my bedtime. Thank you for enduring the long hours of writing and for making sure I was hydrated and had a constant source of caffeine and onion dip. I love you!

In memory of Lane Fitzgerald: you were the epitome of *"Being You,"* even when your outside-of-the-box antics received side glances from Administration. Your belief in me, my CHI and my career potential has always given me the confidence to be better. To Colleen-Joy Page, founder of InnerLifeSkills®, and Yvette Duncan: thank you for the training and mentoring you provided during my Enneagram and Master Coach certification qualifications through the ILS programs. If it weren't for you, I might still think I'm a Type 4! I wouldn't have the entertaining mistyping stories that have inspired others to ditch the Enneagram tests and rely on their own intuition. To Beatrice Chestnut, Ph.D.: thanks for helping me really understand the Countertypes for each of the types, especially for Type 7. That solidified my confidence in my own typing and in coaching others who are struggling to discover or accept their true Core Type.

I'm grateful to Greg, Lea, John, Mark, Allyson, and other friends, students, and clients (whose names and identifying details have been respectfully changed) for the quotes and examples that helped me turn a potentially mind-numbing topic into something more easily understood through your stories.

And finally, an overflowing boatload of appreciation for my editor and coach, Lisa McGrath, and graphics designer, Jacqui Smith, for their support and expertise to pull this book together in spite of the difficult challenges life threw at us. Thank you for your dedication to me and the book through all that. Your encouragement and belief in my vision kept me going when it would have been easy to have just given up.

Ultimately, none of this would have been possible without my faith and my hope of fulfilling the kingdom purpose for which I was created and making a difference in the lives of the readers.

About the Author

Jen P Higgins believes that when you understand her signature holistic approach of problem-solving using proven personality strategies you will feel less drained and more effective at bringing out the best in others, without compromising who you are and what you value. She serves as a Personality Strategist for coaches, educators, and mentors to be the role model you want to be for your students/clients by working with your personality instead of against it.

For over two decades, Jen has coached teams to work well together by helping them align values and goals and teaching them how to communicate with seemingly opposing personalities. From the corporate setting to home-based business owners, she has helped teams be more productive, more confident, and get along better by leveraging the different strengths in the group. She has a private practice working closely with coaches, teachers, and business owners who are looking for work/life balance and the strategies that will motivate and empower them to do what they feel they are called to do.

In 2007, Jen found herself navigating ADHD, Autism, Dyslexia, and the sensory and dietary needs of her family, following fads and expert advice on how to "fix" her children. Jen realized that... just like in the business teams she has helped... Everybody's Different and that difference is not a weakness or a label that defines you. That difference is a superpower unique to you that the world needs and the world only benefits from it when you are being true to yourself.

Jen homeschooled her two sons with this philosophy that you don't need to be fixed, rather you need to explore what makes you different and embrace it. Afterward, Jen taught in the elementary classroom and helped her students learn through questioning and self-regulating exercises, so they would never feel like there was something wrong with them.

After the pandemic hit, Jen moved to the online classroom, but this time to support mentors with courses and group coaching to better understand their personality, or personal individuality, so they can stop comparing themselves to others, discover what makes them unique, and effortlessly serve others from that space.

Jen is the founder of Unbox University, home of the UBU Coach Certification program and UBU Business Mastermind for personal and professional support and accountability. She is an internationally certified Life Coach and Enneagram expert but prefers to be known as the laid-back, fun mom who you can relax with and just *Be You*.

You can find Jen online using the handle *@powercoachjen* and the *Unbox Your Personality* podcast.

Website: go.unboxenneagram.com/goodies

For more information on courses, coaching, and community about the **9 Acknowledgment Languages**™ visit:

Website: UnBoxUni.com

Scan code to download the free
C.O.R.E. framework worksheet